Writing User
Documentation

BCS Practitioner Series

Series editor: Ray Welland

BELINA ET AL   SDL: with applications from protocol specification
BRAEK/HAUGEN   Engineering real time systems
BRINKWORTH   Software quality management: a pro-active approach
CRITCHLEY/BATTY   Open systems – the reality
FOLKES/STUBENVOLL   Accelerated systems development
GIBSON   Managing computer projects: avoiding the pitfalls
HIPPERSON   Practical systems analysis: for users, managers and analysts
LEYLAND   Electronic data interchange
MONK ET AL   Improving your human-computer interface: a practical technique
HORROCKS/MOSS   Practical data administration
THE RAISE LANGUAGE GROUP   The RAISE specification language
RICE   VMS systems management
TANSLEY/HAYBALL   Knowledge based systems analysis and design
VERYARD   Information modelling: practical guidance
VERYARD   Information coordination: the management of information models, systems and organizations
WELLMAN   Software costing

Writing User Documentation

A practical guide for those who want to be read

Roderick Low
with
Harriet Ford
John Pallot
James Hall

Prentice Hall

New York   London   Toronto   Sydney   Tokyo   Singapore

First published in 1994 by
Prentice Hall International (UK) Limited
Campus 400, Maylands Avenue,
Hemel Hempstead,
Hertfordshire, HP2 7EZ
A division of
Simon & Schuster International Group

Printed and bound in Great Britain by
Redwood Books Ltd, Trowbridge, Wilts

Library of Congress Cataloging-in-Publication Data

Writing user documentation : a practical guide for those who want to
    be read / Roderick Low . . . [et al.].
        p.   cm.
    Includes bibliographical references and index.
    ISBN 0-13-336835-1
    1. Electronic data processing documentation.   2. User interfaces
(Computer systems)   I. Low, Roderick.
QA76.9.D6W75   1994
808′.066005–dc20   93-25427
                                                                   CIP

British Library Cataloguing in Publication Data

A catalogue record for this book is available from
the British Library

ISBN 0–13–336835–1 (pbk)

---

1 2 3 4 5   98   97 96 95 94

Contents

Editorial preface ix
Preface xi

1 The psychology of user documentation 1
   1.1   The measure of the problem 1
   1.2   Considering the audience 5
   1.3   Determining the correct book structure 8
   1.4   Reducing reader resistance 12

2 The qualities of a good 'technical' writer 14

3 Investigation - the key to a good result 20
   3.1   The investigation stages 20
   3.2   Considering your audience 21
   3.3   Determining the optimum length of the books 25
   3.4   Looking at the system 26
   3.5   Starting the investigation 30
   3.6   Determining the book titles and types 32
   3.7   Avoiding the pitfalls 32
   3.8   Summary 35

4 Paper based or electronic - the pros and cons of modern technology and the development of on-line manuals 36
   4.1   How we read books and why 36
   4.2   A brief history of on-line text 39
   4.3   Choosing your documentation medium 41

5 The preparation of synopses and styleguides - the synergy of writing and design 43
   5.1   An introduction to the synopsis 44
   5.2   The different aspects to consider 44
   5.3   The style of writing, purpose, and audience 45

5.4	The front matter	45
5.5	The main text	48
5.6	The titling of the books	54
5.7	Preparing the styleguide	54
5.8	Preparing visuals	63
6	Some basic lessons in document design	65
6.1	Corporate standards	65
6.2	Considering the users' environment	66
6.3	Working with the writer	67
6.4	Creating the design	67
6.5	Summary	74
7	Obtaining diagrams and assembling a book	75
7.1	Screens and reports	75
7.2	Other illustrations	79
7.3	Annotation	80
7.4	Assembling the book	80
8	The drafting process - three stages to a satisfactory conclusion	83
8.1	The drafting stages	83
8.2	Who should be involved in the draft review?	84
8.3	What sort of mark-up should you expect to receive from the reviewers?	86
8.4	Dealing with a system still under development	87
8.5	Dealing with a change of reviewer	88
9	Some guidelines for producing effective text	89
9.1	What tools do I need?	89
9.2	Starting to write	90
9.3	Writing style	92
9.4	The front matter	97
9.5	The end matter	102
9.6	Personal editing	107
9.7	Dealing with writer's block	108
9.8	Productivity	109
10	Editing - the vitally necessary evil	111
10.1	Background to the editing task	111
10.2	Who should be the editor?	112
10.3	Initial checks	113
10.4	Editing the appearance/layout	114
10.5	The technical edit	116
10.6	The 'word quality' or 'English' edit	118

10.7 Who should make the corrections?   120
10.8 Editor's marks   121
10.9 Summary   123

11 Maintaining the confidence of the owner   124
11.1 Preliminary discussions   125
11.2 Sign-off documents   125
11.3 General pointers for reviewers   126
11.4 The synopsis and design styleguide   127
11.5 The first draft   128
11.6 The second draft   129
11.7 The final draft   130
11.8 The index   130
11.9 Conclusion   131

12 Management of the documentation process   132
12.1 Defining the production stages   133
12.2 Setting a schedule   136
12.3 Soothing the battered ego   138
12.4 Working with designers, illustrators, and desktop
      publishing operators   139
12.5 Co-ordination and liaison with owners and
      their representatives   140
12.6 Change of reviewer   141
12.7 Conclusion   141

13 Some basic lessons in document production -
    getting books onto shelves   142
13.1 The alternatives   142
13.2 The considerations   146
13.3 A note of caution   149
13.4 Choosing whether to print in-house or externally 150
13.5 Print monitoring   150

14 Writing for export - is language the only problem? 152
14.1 The problems of language   152
14.2 Considerations when writing for translation   156
14.3 How to manage the translation   157
14.4 Translating desktop-published books   160
14.5 Translation of illustrations   160
14.6 Scheduling the translation   161

15 Conclusion   162

Bibliography   164
Glossary   165
Index   169

Editorial preface

The aim of the BCS Practitioner Series is to produce books which are relevant for practising computer professionals across the whole spectrum of Information Technology activities. We want to encourage practitioners to share their practical experience of methods and applications with fellow professionals. We also seek to disseminate information in a form which is suitable for the practitioner who often has only limited time to read widely within a new subject area or to assimilate research findings.

The role of the BCS is to provide advice on the suitability of books for the Series, via the Editorial Panel, and to provide a pool of potential authors upon which we can draw. Our objective is that this Series will reinforce the drive within the BCS to increase professional standards in IT. The other partners in this venture, Prentice Hall, provide the publishing expertise and international marketing capabilities of a leading publisher in the computing field.

The response when we set up the Series was extremely encouraging. However, the success of the Series depends on there being practitioners who want to learn, as well as those who feel they have something to offer! The Series is under continual development and we are always looking for ideas for new topics and feedback on how to improve further the usefulness of the Series. If you are interested in writing for the Series then please contact us.

Documentation is so poor in many parts of the IT industry that it is treated with derision. There is obviously a great challenge to improve the quality of technical documentation as part of the push for higher quality IT systems. This book contains clear practical advice on how to produce good documentation. The author is a professional producer of technical documentation and has distilled his extensive experience into this book. Anybody who has to write any form of documentation should find useful ideas in here. I certainly did!

Ray Welland
Computing Science Department, University of Glasgow

Editorial Panel Members
Frank Bott (UCW, Aberystwyth), John Harrison (BAe Sema), Nic Holt (ICL), Trevor King (Praxis Systems plc), Tom Lake (GLOSSA), Kathy Spur (Analysis and Design Consultants), Mario Wolczko (University of Manchester).

Preface

The first thing you may have noticed about this book is the abundance of text on the cover. I make no apologies for this. After all, you might expect this from a book devoted to the business of generating words. Perhaps, however, the title, subtitle, and credit given to what amounts to a veritable inkwell of writers need an explanation.

This book sets out to explain how to write user documentation. It is not, you will be relieved to read, an English grammar book. Nor does it attempt to progress you from an assumed understanding of grammatical construction to the position where you can lay claim to an impressive writing style.

Everybody thinks they can write, but many who can write do not write particularly well, or do not write appropriately. If, with the honesty box just a little too close for comfort, you admit that writing is not your forte, you may use this book to set standards for others to follow. If you can write, but feel frustrated by the results you obtain, you may gain much on a personal level.

This leads me to the subtitle of the book. The only real measure of a well-written user document is that it is read. Further, that it is read by individuals who quickly recognise with a growing sense of confidence that they understand what is written.

Writing good user documentation is, first and foremost, about wanting to be read. It must not be a chore - the tail-end Charlie of a job just before the launch of a project. It should not be used, or seen, as nothing more than a necessary evil. And the writing exercise is not primarily about the project, service, or system, described therein. It is about the readers - the audience if you like. It is about what they have to know and what they have to do.

You may be puzzled by the fact that the names of four authors appear on the cover with nothing more than a little preposition establishing some hinted-at hierarchy. Was it really written by four people?, I hear you asking. Well, not really. I wrote the book, but what I wrote is not entirely or exactly what you are reading. In addition to the professional editing skills of Prentice Hall, the publishers (for which profound thanks, incidentally), and the advice of the editorial panel under the guiding hand of the British Computer Society, my colleagues (those whose names follow the 'with') have provided the illustrations, selected the examples, reminded me of the experiences that form the basis of the case studies, scoffed at my witty comments in which they vainly sought the wit, shaken their heads at convoluted arguments that, like the horrors of school-day equations, do not resolve themselves neatly, and tried their best to provide editing skills that, if nothing else, kept my sentences down to a reasonable length.

Oh, you noticed. That last sentence ran to one hundred and twelve words. Far too long. You see, writing a book on how to write user documentation gives one a golden opportunity to include examples of the mistakes people make. So, while we hope you will read this book through like a novel - hardly stopping to eat or to sleep - we intend to provide the odd faux pas - a chunk of turgid text here, an explanation as clear as the smog of 1952 there - just to keep you on your toes.

It is our belief that no single individual can write a piece of user documentation. There should always be, consequently, several 'withs'. This being the case, we decided that this book should be written in the same way as a piece of user documentation. Indeed, it is only vanity that has driven me to establish my name at the head of the list. Writing this book, like writing all the user documentation my company develops for its clients, has been a collaborative process. No single individual in our organisation 'owns' a user guide. And so it is with this book.

Although I wrote the original script, the words were changed out of all recognition by my colleagues. They acted as technical and text editors - people you will read about in the ensuing chapters. One of our number is a book designer, so he took the established style of the BCS Practitioner Series and battered my words and ideas into a format that Prentice Hall's benign and over-tolerant Acquisitions Editor, Viki Williams, on a day of exceptional charity, passed for publication.

If this book achieves its goal, by the time you reach the index you will appreciate what it takes to write readable text. The rest will be up to you.

I hope you will forgive me on one point. I have to refer to the people involved in the documentation process at various stages throughout the book, and have come up against the dilemma of gender. Just occasionally, I have slipped into the trap of assuming the masculine to refer to both men and women. I hope my female readers will forgive me for this shabby solution to one of the excruciating difficulties in the English language.

Like most books, *Writing User Documentation* is divided into a number of chapters. These are described in outline below.

Chapter 1 - The psychology of user documentation

This chapter sets the scene for the balance of the book by making you aware of the purpose behind the provision of documentation. It draws some embarrassing parallels with situations in which documentation has worked in the past and present - in other industries. It also sets the parameters within which the good technical writer must work if he or she is to be successful.

Chapter 2 - The qualities of a good technical writer

Although being able to express oneself clearly and concisely on paper is valuable, there are a number of other abilities that I would suggest are just as important. These are outlined before we get down to the business of discussing the writing process in detail.

Chapter 3 - Investigation - the key to a good result

The novelist thinks of a plot and then begins to write. For a writer of user documentation, the investigation that leads to a good document is as much about the audience as it is about the product or service it sets out to explain. This chapter outlines the approach to be adopted, and includes some tips that will help the writer to ensure the success of the investigation.

Chapter 4 - Paper-based or electronic - the pros and cons of modern technology and the development of on-line manuals

This chapter wheels all the starry-eyed technology arguments out of the door, and looks in a dispassionate way at the new approaches. Some conclusions are, however, drawn that are not entirely Luddite in sentiment.

Chapter 5 - The preparation of synopses and styleguides - the synergy of text and design

If documentation is to appeal to readers with a broad span of knowledge, the involvement of illustration and good design is essential. 'A picture is worth a thousand words,' so they say. This chapter shows how a writing style is changed by the incorporation of stylistic techniques. It also stresses the importance of a carefully researched synopsis.

Chapter 6 - Some basic lessons in document design

Many topics, such as page layout, intelligent use of white space, structure, paper size, desktop publishing, captions, italics, and spot colour, are discussed in this chapter.

Chapter 7 - Obtaining diagrams and assembling a book

This chapter describes the different types of illustration you may wish to include in a book. It examines the thinking behind good diagram design and then explores some of the products that are here to help us when compiling a book.

Chapter 8 - The drafting process - three stages to a satisfactory conclusion

Accuracy and input from the owner are essential elements in the production of any book. This chapter describes the different stages through which a book should progress, and the opportunity for the owner's nominated representatives to review the content at each stage.

Chapter 9 - Some guidelines for producing effective text

The major part of most user guides is words. This chapter provides some guidelines about how to set about the writing processes and describes in detail the content of some essential elements of the book.

Chapter 10 - Editing - the vitally necessary evil

No room for egos in the professional writing business. Editors have final say in the content of the book. Their task is described in this chapter.

Chapter 11 - Maintaining the confidence of the owner

Although the books are for a specific audience, the writer is ultimately working for the company owning the book. This chapter provides some ideas about ensuring the owner is kept happy.

Chapter 12 - Management of the documentation process

Forget the lonely garret bordering the 7th arrondissement, with inspiration coming from the scent of new-baked bread. Professional writing is a production process - a manufacture - quite appropriate to the tenets of BS5750. This chapter summarises the key points in the documentation process and the way in which projects must be managed to ensure that they are completed to the satisfaction of all parties.

Chapter 13 - Some basic lessons in document production - getting books onto shelves

Although most user guides nowadays are desktop-published, there are still a number of routes that may be followed to achieve the final printed version. Some obvious errors can be committed at this last vital stage. This chapter describes how to avoid some of the worst mistakes.

Chapter 14   -   Writing for export - is language the only problem?

'Please quay the appropriate individual into the first meadow on the screen' is a poor translation of 'please key the appropriate character into the first field on the screen', but this is not the only type of howler to avoid if your documentation is to be translated. Increasingly, software products are crossing political and linguistic barriers. This chapter discusses the problems of quality of translation and coping with cultural objections and provides a few solutions.

Chapter 15   -   Conclusion

Just a few final words about the writing process.

This book includes a glossary, which should be of value to practising writers, and an index. Glossaries and indexes are very important adjuncts to good user documentation, so the practical development of these will be described.

Documentation is, of course, a very broad subject and constraints of length have necessarily restricted this publication to a discussion of user documentation. Tasks such as documenting technical software, maintaining documents and technical descriptions of document design are all major subjects in their own right. As such, these are not included in this book.

It only remains for me to thank everyone who has helped in the development of this book and also to thank you for reading thus far. I, and my colleagues, hope that you will enjoy and benefit from the experiences of one technical writer who is still learning.

Roderick Low
Ashwell, Hertfordshire

1   The psychology of user documentation

User documentation developed to describe computer systems and services has a terrible reputation. When people ask me what I do for a living, it takes all my courage to say that I write computer manuals. Indeed, it is not unusual for me to hide, yellow-bellied, behind my directorial title or to murmur something about being 'in computers'.

Just as the general practitioner who reveals his calling at a dinner party will spend the rest of the evening diagnosing the sundry real or imagined ills of his fellow guests, so, when I have had the courage to be honest, I feel I must quickly follow it with an apologetic justification for my inclusion, albeit at a subordinate level, within the human race. And yet I enjoy writing documentation and find it hard to convince the sceptical of the fact that the documentation that I and my colleagues write is liked, used, and, to my bank manager's intense relief, paid for.

Clearly, something is rotten in the state of Denmark. The received opinion of many armchair critics is supported by abundant evidence all around us.

1.1   The measure of the problem

With computer companies now the world's biggest publishers, the preparation of computer documentation is clearly a vast industry. But it is one that is largely overshadowed by the subject matter. A computer is measured by its power, its compatibility, its speed, its reliability, and by its willingness to be upgraded. It does not rely on the quality of its documentation for its popularity. Likewise, applications software is measured by how robust it is, by the extent of its features, by how well it is supported, and, once again, not by the quality of its documentation.

And so, the computer documentation industry stumbles on - largely avoiding proper critical acclaim and almost universally the butt of derision. In the documentation industry's defence, it should be pointed out that it can trace its ancestry to a time when the audience was small and, in a technological sense, highly skilled. Computers of twenty years ago and more were managed by technicians and fed by the long-suffering occupants of the punch room. To the general public, computer manuals only really became a factor in their lives with the advent of the personal computer. After decades of misinforming the few who fortunately hardly needed informing at all, the computer documentation industry was let loose on Joe Public.

And yet the poor quality documentation for computer users cannot, surely, be mirrored in the oil, defence, or aircraft industries? They have manuals upon which lives depend, and so they cannot afford the luxury of imprecision, inaccuracy, and inappropriateness. Other industries have also been getting it right for a very long time.

In 1895, Sir William Armstrong, Mitchell and Company, a Newcastle upon Tyne shipbuilder, was contracted to build an ice-breaking trainferry to ply the waters of Lake Baikal in Siberia. The intrepid Tynesiders built the ship, all 290 feet of her, as they would any other ship, on Tyneside. They also subcontracted the building of the engines, boilers, and pumps to a firm in St Petersburg. Then, after manufacture of the hull and fitting out and without sight of the mechanical parts, the ship, to be named, not surprisingly, 'Baikal', was dismantled for transportation. Ship and engines (also dismantled after building and testing) were united at St Petersburg and 7,000 components were transported by rail, river, and sledge to the shores of the lake. There, with the assistance of a marine engineer and four foremen from the Tyne, a set of engineering drawings, and one or two manuals detailing the components and their assembly, she was literally reconstructed and entered service in April 1900.

There is no doubting the competence of those five Tynesiders, but to assume that, between them, they knew all there was to know about a ship - a third of which they had not even seen in the building - is to beggar belief. The documentation - much of it in Russian - was an essential element in the exercise. Although the building of a railway around the southern shores of Lake Baikal rendered the trainferrying capabilities of the ship redundant shortly afterwards, 'Baikal' and her smaller sister the 'Angara', built and assembled in the same way, continued to ply the lake as conventional ferries for many years - the 'Baikal' being destroyed during the Revolution. The 'Angara' was certainly still in existence in 1977 and may still survive - a fine example of the ability to perform complex tasks with a little knowledge and good documentation.

Now, if it was possible nearly a hundred years ago to document such a complicated process, and many other industries today have no problems with setting down complex processes in writing, why is this not possible in the computer industry? Why cannot already skilled production controllers, storemen, accounts clerks and the like make the small step from manual methods or a redundant computer system to a new set-up without confusion, error, loss of confidence, emotional irrationality, and unforeseen expense?

Without having had sight of the building instructions for the 4,250-ton 'Baikal', I would like to suggest the following probabilities.

The instructions for building 'Baikal' will have been written in a style and language familiar to those who had to read them. While they will have contained technical terms, there will not have been one that was not as familiar to the audience as the fields, screens, and processors of our argot. The Russian documentation describing the engines and boilers - certain technical features of which would not have been familiar to the British, since 'Baikal' was a woodburner - would similarly have been couched in terms that Russian engineers and interpreters could cope with.

Furthermore, the instructions will have been set out in an orderly way - the words and diagrams following the process through from identification of each component (7,000 remember!) to assembly and testing. To undertake such a task, the instructions will have been concise and to the point. Not for them, seven thousand words describing the standards expected of the EC sausage skin! Or the two million words apparently needed to explain a mainframe accounting system from a UK software house, or the 30 volumes needed to support £18,000.00 worth of mid-range computer.

Those engineers of long ago did not have the luxury of being able to assume that no one would actually read the documentation - or that its mere presence, however turgid or inaccurate, would satisfy the users. Every word, every diagram, every event in the process, had to be understood. If it was not, the ship would not have been completed.

Delays caused by the weather and the problem of getting the boilers to the lakeside *are* on record. What is not recorded are any delays caused by misunderstandings at the assembly site or, most familiar to those involved in the computer industry, delays caused by the owner or user realising that what he was getting was not what he wanted. Therefore, we may assume that the specifications as well as the assembly and user instructions met the bill - nearly one hundred years ago.

This 'Baikal' story is, of course, not unique. Vast feats involving the skills of individuals, together with accurate and unambivalent documentation, have taken place since the dawn of the industrial revolution. It is frankly embarrassing to think of the assembly of the Statue of Liberty, the building of the Panama Canal (the second time around!), and pure writing tasks such as the drafting of the American Constitution, and compare these with some of the computer industry blunders of our times, caused, or at least contributed to, by poor documentation.

In the context of the computer industry, we must recognise, in these more thoughtful nineties, that the control of waste is not simply a Green issue. Poor user documentation can cause waste beyond comprehension, in the same way as careless system design, lack of recognition of what is really required, inaccurate specification, and bad training.

So, what can we learn from those engineers of long ago? What made their efforts successful and lasting, while ours are often disappointing and ephemeral?

At this point, I could be accused of trying to compare like with unlike. It could be argued that the 'Baikal' documentation was of a fairly technical nature and, by and large, *technical* computer documentation is fairly good - pitched at the right level, addressed to the specific audience, complete, accurate, and so on. Point taken. But if this is so, it shows that the computer industry *per se* can get it right in one department while getting it lamentably wrong in another. All the more reason for asking the questions, therefore.

Of course, there is a danger that questions about the successes of the past and the failures of the present result in the revelation of a canvas that is not only too large, but beyond the scope of this book. It is difficult, for instance, to write good user documentation set against a background of a project that is running late, underfunded, badly managed, and that has already lost the confidence of the potential user community. Similarly, it is hard to develop good documentation when no budget has been specifically set aside for this important element. Few software companies would admit to including a figure representing 10 per cent of software development costs for documentation, and yet this is probably a conservative estimate which rises exponentially as we talk of smaller projects, i.e. anything below a capital cost of £500,000.

However sophisticated the techniques employed and however skilled the writers, a documentation project that is underfunded or which is required yesterday will turn out poorly. The writing process needs time and it has to be paid for. There is, of course, a profound obverse to this, but the benefits - good understanding, reduced error and help-desk workload, a competitive edge, and more rapid implementation - are all difficult to quantify and 'in the future'.

Hopefully, some of the other titles in this BCS Practitioner series of books will lead to greater professionalism in the planning and execution of projects. Whether the Achilles' heel of documentation - particularly user documentation - will be fully recognised for the contribution it can make both to the success *and* failure of projects is another matter.

I must, however, avoid getting into circumlocutory diatribes about the need for overall project planning and the establishment of adequate budgets before a successful writing project can be commenced. Let it just be said, and said no more, that these are essential, and that anyone imagining that wonderful documentation can emanate from an impoverished project is allowing wishful thinking to separate them from reality. I know from my professional experience as a writer and as head of a small writing company that, despite strenuous efforts to the contrary, we produce very good books for very good products and services and less good books for products and services that are less than perfect. It is a hard thing to admit but, to an extent, products and services get the books they deserve.

Fortunately, however, there are many companies which exercise strict project control and recognise the benefits that may be accrued from good customer or internal user support. This, in the form of proper training facilities, on-site and help-desk support, on-line help that really does help, *and* documentation, is tending to drive a wedge between the enlightened organisations and those who bluff their way through. There are now, in effect, two kinds of computer system user or supplier - those that see benefit in nurturing value for money out of their investments, and those that insist upon it, demand it, but do nothing to make certain of it.

All is not lost, therefore, but in my estimation the time is ripe for a minor revolution in the computer industry. Until we can easily and cheaply put reasonable understanding into the minds of those who hold the key to success or failure in the use of computer systems, the disappointments will continue.

So what makes for good user documentation?

To some extent the answers have already been hinted at - the appropriateness of the 'Baikal's' assembly instructions and the avoidance of 'technospeak' unless it is universally understood by all the potential readership, and the need for clarity, brevity, and accuracy.

Easier said than done, of course. We can all go on, and on, and on, and on, about the things that interest us, losing all balance and objectivity. We can certainly write for ourselves - and many novelists say that, although the cheques and fame are quite nice, they try to please themselves before the audience. But there is no place for this kind of approach in documenting computer systems. In addition, the writer of user documentation has even greater obstacles to overcome than those of the conventional technical author - such as writers of aircraft manuals and even 'Baikal's' documenters.

1.2   Considering the audience

Rarely would a production controller in a manufacturing establishment admit that the user guide for his computerised production control system makes even the smallest contribution to his performance as a production controller. This is not true of the aircraft engineer - he would say that the skills learned over many years combined with the documentation for the latest engine or landing gear were the prerequisites of success in his job. The production controller often sees the user guide for his computer system as yet another thing to get in the way of his instinctive eye and consummate experience in the job. The aircraft engineer, on the other hand, carries his manual with pride. To the analogy of production controllers, we may add almost anyone who has to use a modern commercial computer. The credit controller, the sales manager, the water company official, the bank clerk, the fuel oil distributor, the quality controller, the foodstuffs chemist - all learned their profession or trade with a dependence on, rather than an interest in, the computer.

Have you noticed how often manuals for mainframe and mid-range computers are held in A4 binders and how big they are? It is quite easy for a user guide to reach 400 pages with 200 words on each page - 80,000 words. The text is rarely relieved by diagrams and, where it is, the relief commonly takes the form of an impression of a screen. The surrounding area of the screen is often established by a box of pretty asterisks and the contents of the screen distorted to accommodate the text in whatever font is to hand. The subject of design is pursued further later in this chapter and discussed more fully later in this book, but let us just think what these great literary dinosaurs are intended to do.

These user guides are intended for the edification of the user, so let us examine some typical users. If our 400 page, 80,000 word manual is to be read by computer experts, that is not so bad. They, at least, are used to such tomes. But consider an accountant. What will he, or she, make of the book? An accountant tends to be quite a logical creature, so he turns to the contents sheet to identify which part of the book contains information about carrying forward balances and closing down ledgers at the year-end. Alas, no contents sheet or, if there is one, headings so vague that he cannot relate what he wants to the words on the page. Some contents sheets, by contrast, are so long that they practically need contents sheets of their own. I once saw one of 16 pages.

So our accountant starts to thumb through the manual, but he is already irritated. Is it him? Is he stupid because he cannot find what he is looking for? Well of course he isn't, but maybe he is beginning to think he is and that is very bad news for the computer system supplier. This inward sense of inadequacy from senior people usually manifests itself in criticism of the product or service out of all proportion to its shortcomings.

Now think in terms of the user being a seventeen-year-old clerk. He or she does not read very much at all. They get almost all they need from the television and from very accessible sociable forms of entertainment. Reading is limited to directories for their forms of relaxation - newspapers, TV and radio magazines, music papers, etc. So we give him or her 80,000 words between dull blue covers and tell them to 'do it', with some vague promise of help if they need it.

They don't, of course, say they won't. And they probably do their best, but they learn most things from habit, not from the academic approach. So, some months later, by asking lots of questions and reading tiny isolated parts of the book, they have learned to do their job. That is to say, they can do their job 'spinally' - information in at one end, results out at the other. They do not know why they do their job insofar as it is reflected on the computer, only how to do it. This gap in their understanding can be ably met by the writing of a short and encouraging systems overview - but how many systems are accompanied by an overview?

In addition, these users often do not have any understanding of the side-pieces of the system - the 'ribs' if you like - the aspects that were so much a part of the specification or the decision to buy the system in the first place. Nor can they properly interpret the information on the screen, seeing the computer as a nuisance, not as an aid to their work.

And this perception of computers - awkward things that are a nuisance rather than a help - is not restricted to young clerks whose ears are still ringing from the Wembley concert last Saturday. The accountant and the production controller may see more benefit, but their honest appraisal of the contribution the system makes to their responsibilities within the organisation may be smaller than you imagine.

Of course, we in the computer industry know that this kind of perception is wrong. Hundreds of man years of experience go into system development. Proper consultative procedures are undertaken to ensure that, by and large, the computer can deliver what is required. Whole industries now rely totally on computers to provide processes at a speed that simply could not be emulated by human beings - no matter how many Canary Wharves they occupied. Imagine trading in bonds without computers. Or credit card systems without computers. Or booking airline tickets without computers.

So, there is a great gulf between perception and reality. And the gap between the two is maintained by a steady torrent of misunderstandings on both sides, spinal use of computers, errors, and misinterpretation leading to bad (and expensive!) decisions.

The only way to bridge the gap is to find ways of improving understanding on the part of the user. This, in turn, will ensure that the suggestions and criticisms made by the user community will be informed and accurate, and the systems can be enhanced to match the changing requirements of the users.

This improvement in understanding will come partly from better training courses but, to my mind, their benefits are rather short-term. A course generally takes place in a rarefied atmosphere, usually at breakneck speed, and not everyone will have the benefit of having been on the course. The effect of this is to restrict the flow of ideas and information in a single direction - from tutor to student. For those in the modern gypsy society we call the mobile working population, there is a tendency for people to change jobs and for the new recruits to miss out on specific system training. In all but the most professional organisations, training comes in with a bang and goes out with a whimper. As a consequence, genuine understanding and positive criticism of a system can only come over a longer period, and the nourishment for this kind of growth in understanding must come from good documentation

Above all, therefore, we must write for the audience. Theirs will be a hostile read. We must win them over. Theirs will be a selfish read. We must give them what they want. Our task is not to educate or waste their time. Our task is to inform at their level - not to patronise, but to meet them and their needs with a degree of modesty. Unless we can start to achieve more accurate use of computer systems on a wider scale, the good intentions of the bottlebank user will be quite overwhelmed by corporate waste of what we might term computocash - the money spent on and administered by computers.

This is not to say that we must produce magazine-like manuals for clerks, legalistic manuals for company secretaries, or ones that resemble the Pirelli calendar for the production control area. But we must write for the audience. This means fragmentation of the overall product or service description into audience type. Many manuals contain information for computer operators alongside genuine user guide material. It is not uncommon to find back-up and restore instructions knee-deep in customer record addition and amendment. This must all change.

1.3   Determining the correct book structure

One of the keys to determining the different types of audience for a series of books is having an understanding of the way information is used in a company. Essentially there are three elements to this (see Figure 1.1).

The basic information store for the company consists of the source information held on file and made available to various departments as required. For example, customer details would need to be available to the sales team (when taking an order), the despatch department (to know where to send the goods), and the accounts department (to raise the invoice and ensure that payment is received).

Figure 1.1
The basic information store for the company

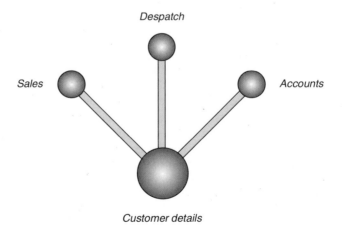

Despatch

Sales

Accounts

Customer details

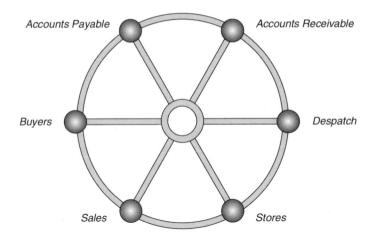

Figure 1.2
The way in which
information is passed
between departments

The second element is the way in which the information is passed between departments (see Figure 1.2). This may occur in a straight-line fashion, but is more likely to follow a complex network of paths, depending on circumstances arising. For example, and for the sake of argument, if the sales department takes an order, the details will be passed to stores to issue the goods. From there the information is passed, with the goods, to the despatch department. Finally, when despatch has taken place, the details will be passed to the accounts department. However, side-tracks could be made from this path. For example, if the customer is on credit-hold, reference would have to be made to the accounts department before goods can be despatched.

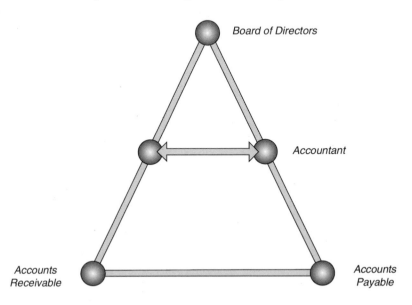

Figure 1.3
The way in which
information is passed up
the management 'ladder'

Figure 1.3 illustrates the third element - the way in which information is passed up the management 'ladder'. In most circumstances, departments pass information upwards and it tends to be refined and reduced at each step up. For example, in a busy accounts department the accountant will not be interested in the day-to-day business of the department, processing invoices and the payments. He will, however, require sufficient information to enable him to compile the company accounts, including information about accounts badly overdue that might become bad debts. Similarly, the directors of the company will not require the detailed background to the accounts, just a summary in the form of the trading account and balance sheet.

If you put all these elements together, you can see that information does not just flow in straight lines. Instead, you must take as a model a three-dimensional structure. We call this the Information CAGE (Information Communication and Generation Expression) (Figure 1.4).

What we have described thus far can be applied to any company, whether operating manual or computerised systems. Clearly, where several people have access to a piece of information, they may use it in different ways depending on their departmental or management responsibilities. Where the system is held on a computer, there may be additional concerns. For example, there may well be a department or person specifically responsible for ensuring the smooth day-to-day operation of the computer. In addition, when the computer is installed, there will be an extensive set-up task to ensure that the information base is transferred successfully into the computer records.

So for a typical computer installation, the set-up instructions, day-to-day operational instructions for the computer people, file maintenance, overviews for management, financial controls, and guidance for specific users - stock controllers, sales people, accountants, credit controllers, despatchers - should be separated and published in different books. As they are being written for different audiences, they can be written in quite different ways - crisp and matter-of-fact for the professional, supportive and encouraging for those not familiar with computers, technical - in the computer sense - where support of the system is the subject, and technical - in the users' understanding of the term - where that is appropriate.

The other benefit of this fragmentation process is the fact that each book can now be much shorter, which makes everyone's reading matter enormously more approachable.

Finally and most importantly, the manuals should be written from the point of view of the readers and the tasks they wish to perform. The way this can be achieved requires a great deal of explanation and the qualities needed to achieve this will be discussed in the next chapter. It is much easier, given a computer system with fixed menus, to list all the options in the contents sheet and describe the operation of each one systematically. But this turns the user guide around from being about the job to being about the computer system - and this is fundamentally wrong.

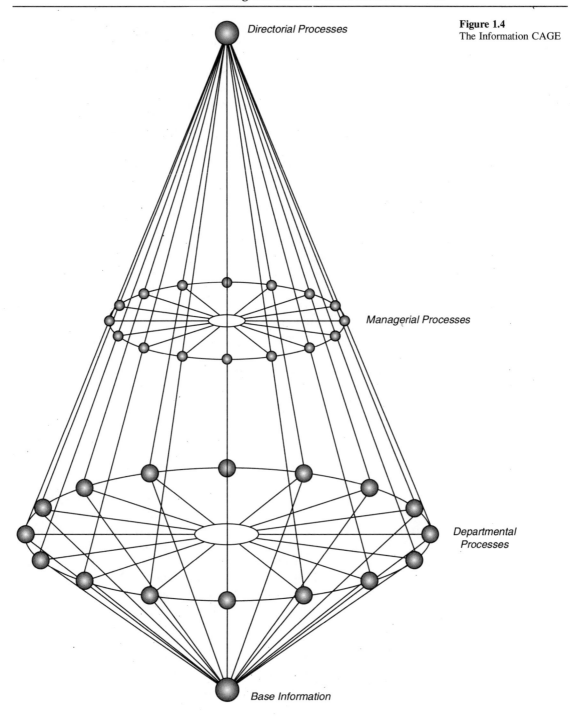

Directorial Processes

Managerial Processes

Departmental
Processes

Base Information

Figure 1.4
The Information CAGE

If we are to win the hearts and minds of the users so that computer systems and services are to be used correctly and economically, we must give them entirely, and only, what they need.

1.4   Reducing reader resistance

There are just a few other points I would like to raise at this stage. Having structured your books to suit the audience, you have begun to fight the battle, but you have not yet won the vote of your readers. It is vitally important that, having received the book most appropriate to their job, the reader finds the content readable and accurate.

Any user finding a factual error in a manual, particularly in the early stage of becoming familiar with its use, is likely to distrust it from that moment on. Similarly, if a user finds errors of omission, they are likely to stop using the manual on the basis that the information they require is not likely to be found in it. Both are quite understandable reactions from those who are busy with their day-to-day jobs and want the computer to be a help and not a hindrance.

Whilst ensuring that you provide enough information in each manual, you must also avoid writing too much. You must make sure that all the information you provide is clear and concise. Any user having to wade through reams of irrelevant description will soon lose heart and turn to the help line instead. Later chapters of this book illustrate ways in which you can achieve this careful balance.

One final point is the appearance of the finished book. Almost all professional writers use word processing systems to develop text. The transition from putting words down on paper to keying them into a computer may take a little while to perfect but, after a while, the use of a word processor for mass development of text becomes second nature and writing letters to Great Aunt Agatha on the old Bond seems strange.

The argument for desktop publishing user guides (or emulating desktop publishing features through a word processor) is overwhelming and really the only type of document which might be more appropriate in traditional word-processed form would be a set of very dynamic standards and procedures. In this case, adding an additional layer of maintenance to be carried out in the form of desktop publishing each time there is a minor change may become prohibitive in terms of time and expenditure. So practical reasons might inhibit the use of desktop publishing, but little else.

As a non-user of desktop publishing myself (I am fortunate to have a colleague who devotes himself to this work), I can readily appreciate the fact that proficient use of such a system is a valuable skill in itself. To be able merely to 'wind the handle' against an existing stylesheet is clever enough, but most owners either have an existing style or require one to be developed on their behalf.

This requires extra knowledge and a very good book designer's eye if the job is to be perfect. Some 'amateurs' do very well, so long as the style is kept simple, but others try too hard, and end up with too many clashing font types and a structure that is difficult to manage from the point of view of the writing team, and too difficult for the owner and the user of the finished book to understand. The whole point about good design is that it should make a strong contribution to good understanding, so bad design defeats this objective.

Better sometimes that the book be left as a word-processed document, but that is a shame because it is a good opportunity lost.

2 The qualities of a good 'technical' writer

While it would be convenient to list the qualities of a writer of user documentation in the space of a single page and then move swiftly on to meatier topics in subsequent chapters, to do so would have the effect of 'glossing over' an important and complex factor. I will therefore spend some time looking at the thorny subject of writer qualities in the context of the preparation of user documentation.

To begin with, the title 'technical' writer is a bit of a misnomer. It implies that the writer must have a detailed inner knowledge of the computer system, the programming language used to develop it, or, at the very least, an in-depth knowledge of the processes the system has been developed to assist. Not so. Providing you have a good understanding of how businesses operate, an enquiring mind, the ability to think on your feet, and learn quickly, you may have a positive advantage if you do not have any of this prior knowledge. After all, if you have to place yourself in the position of the naive user of the system, how better to do so than as a naive user yourself.

To a large extent, writers are born and not made. As a consequence, it is possible to see potential writers in all walks of life, most of whom will never write a single line for money in their lives. There is a peculiar pleasure to be gained by some of us from setting down words on paper and it doesn't matter whether it is a business letter, a shopping list, or a note to the milkman, a chore it certainly isn't.

This is not to say that writing always comes easy to a professional writer. Although I am only into the fourth paragraph in this chapter, I have been working on it for over an hour and a half, and this is my third draft. Writing is an art form and it is very difficult to force the words out on a nine to five-thirty, five days a week basis if the chemicals in the brain are not mixing in the right ratios. With practice, being able to write 'to order' comes easier and I don't altogether subscribe to the chat-show cliché where the author of a blockbuster rabbits on about staring at the empty page, but it is never completely painless.

So, if you are someone who takes profuse notes, bemoans the telephone-inspired redundancy of true letter writing, is a closet poet, or did, some time ago, start to write a novel that never got beyond a synopsis or perhaps the first chapter, you might be hiding a real talent - the talent to want to write.

Proficiency in writing, of course, can be measured in different ways. Some years ago, educationalists decided that grammar, punctuation, and spelling should not get in the way of the flow of ideas. This approach followed my own formative years where the endless drawing of patterns with a pencil and later a dip-pen in the reception class at school (to develop a good 'hand' they said .... where did it go?), was followed by years of grammar and sentence analysis that would drive all but the most determined to distraction. Goodness knows what the priorities are now, but overall competence at expressing oneself on paper is probably no better or worse than it has ever been.

Someone who is good at spelling may not necessarily be good at writing, and, conversely plenty of good writers are dreadful spellers. Spelling is a sort of trick and in a language with as many ancestral sources as English, good spelling says a great deal about the speller's memory and very little else. Even the old spelling rules, 'i before e, except after c', for example, invariably have exceptions - and not always with foreign (geddit?) words.

Anyway, nowadays poor spelling does not preclude you from becoming a writer of user documentation as word processors are universally equipped with spell-checking devices. However, it should be remembered that some spell-checkers still have an annoying habit of displaying American parentage. This can give the most English of sentences a surprisingly hard edge, especially if you include such words as 'analyze'.

Punctuation and grammar are more of a problem and they are not so easily solved by technology, as the syntax-checkers are not, nor probably ever will be, a wholly effective substitute.

Attitudes to punctuation are going through a period of transition at the present which many of us find difficult. I was brought up at a time when punctuation was seen as a device for assisting in the reading process (a count of 'one' for a comma, 'two' for a full stop, 'three' for a new paragraph). Consequently, punctuation was seen as a positive contributor to understanding.

Nowadays however it seems entirely acceptable even by such upholders of writing standards as the quality press to banish the comma which I feel is so valuable wherever possible. I shall continue to use the comma freely, feeling exonerated by the words of Laurence Sterne in *Tristram Shandy*, namely, 'writing is but a form of conversation'. If you try to read aloud my sentence above that refers to the quality press without pausing, the meaning, I guarantee, will be lost on the listener.

One of the underlying rules when writing user documentation is to keep things simple. While I may, while writing this book, indulge in convoluted sentences that are peppered with subordinate clauses, each needing some punctuation to signal their arrival and departure, this style would be inappropriate in a user document. Of course, the shorter the sentences and the simpler the ideas they contain, the less you need to worry about punctuation. This should not mean that the journalistic style of certain Sunday papers should be adopted ('Something dreadful happened in Greenock last night. There was a murder. It was dreadful.'), but you cannot fault the simplicity of the sentences, the clarity of the message, or the accuracy of the punctuation. Examples of style are to be found in subsequent chapters, and these will provide you with at least some guidance to writing user documentation.

I indicated in the Preface that this was not to be a grammar book and I will keep my promise. However, let me just dwell for a line or two on one tricky little trap into which even the most competent technical writers sometimes fall. This is the knotty area of tense - past, present, future, and so on. Fortunately, only the most particular Oxford scholars now tut, tut, tut, over a drifting away from Latin constructions, so we may not lose too much sleep about how imperfect our pluperfects are.

Nevertheless, you do not have to look too hard on the shelves of computer user guides before you find such as the following:

```
When you select option ten on the menu, the
next screen will be displayed:

You should follow the instructions provided
overleaf to complete the screen.

Please note. If you did not confirm
acceptance of the information by pressing
F4, the database record will not be updated.
```

A person with an aptitude for writing user documentation would be able to spot with little difficulty what is wrong with this piece.

So there are ways around the problems of spelling and, by keeping things simple, you will not have to learn the correct use of the semicolon or the gerund. Unfortunately, while being able to write fluently is important, being good at sentence construction does not alone a good writer of user documentation make, and the professional writer must either acquire or already have many other qualities in their kitbag.

The documenter of user guides has a responsibility to explain to a sometimes sceptical audience how they should undertake their job in the context of some new system or approach. Almost invariably, there is some form of time and/or cost constraint to challenge this objective.

There is, therefore, very little time available to the writer to establish his credentials and start to produce the goods. If you accept my premise that user documentation is more concerned with the reader and his or her objectives than it is with the subject matter of the book itself, you must appreciate the fact that the writer is set a very difficult task.

It is vital for good writers to practise clearing their minds of previous experiences in order to see the world from the point of view of their audience. Above all, user guides must be practical - in other words, they must be 'usable' in a real situation. A true understanding of what is required, and how best to satisfy that requirement, comes from a detailed investigation of the circumstances under which the documentation will be used. Investigation is such an important subject that it merits a chapter of its own in this book.

It goes without saying that investigation means interviewing as well as observing and a good interviewer has specific personal qualities that must be encouraged. Above all, a good interviewer is a good listener. If the interviewer does not listen carefully to the interviewed and alter the course of questioning in the light of what is said, much valuable information will be lost.

To side-track for a moment and provide an example of what I am talking about, when British television first heard of the chat-show concept, all sorts of ill-equipped and ill-informed people filled our living rooms with tedious interviews of the great and the good.

While a few of the 'hosts' were, admittedly, very competent, most seemed too much in awe of their guests to ask any real questions of import. Instead, they measured their success by keeping the film star, playwright, sports personality or politician, talking for the allotted period about their fantastic careers, while looking hopefully, like a devoted labrador, for a little reflected glory. To get a 'well, you know yourself, being in the public eye ...' from an American actress, was like manna to our interviewer, who would beam uncontrollably and nod in superior empathy.

But, so often, the chat-show host demonstrated his impoverished skills when the guest dropped something in that was not expected. Here is a typical, although entirely fictitious, example.

During a monumentally tedious catalogue of films that our craggy old actor has appeared in, the host points out a gap of five years in his otherwise full and brilliant career. The actor, sipping BBC water and well-infected by the host's irritating habit of crossing and uncrossing his legs every seventeen seconds, explains the gap in his career by a statement about an unfortunate business with a shotgun and his fourth wife's lover.

The host raises his eyebrows, looks off-camera to the idiot board, bridges the gap with 'Really. Oh. That's interesting.' and then goes straight on with 'And then you went on to make *Last Train From Duluth* with Ernest Borgnine.'

The only interesting anecdote that could not be found by private study of a compendium of film sketches is completely lost because the interviewer is not really interviewing at all. Even in our lowly station as writers of user documentation, we must learn to ask, listen and, if need be, alter our line of questioning in the light of what we hear.

Furthermore, the good interviewer will gain something from the way that the responses are couched. All sorts of politics and intrigue will come out in a good interview and this background information will help the writer to see what has to be achieved by his document.

The questioning techniques used must make the interviewee relaxed and confident. There is always a real chance that the arrival of a questioning stranger is seen as 'someone up there posing a threat'. This must be overcome by a willingness to empathise with the interviewee and also explain the purpose of the meeting. It is, in short, so that the writer can gain an understanding of the interviewee's job, so that the documentation can be written from the future user's point of view.

Of course, in order to get the most from an interview, it is essential to couch questions in a form and manner that the interviewee will understand. The object of the exercise is to obtain accurate and authoritative information. Both interviewer and interviewee are on the same side. Nothing is calculated to irritate an individual more than questions that put accurate answers out of reach. Superiority on the part of an interviewer quickly looks like a threat and if the supplier of the information goes onto the defensive, there is very little chance of the interview being successful. On the other hand, staying in the placid waters of the banal may keep everyone happy, but it will not result in a transfer of knowledge from those who know to those who would like to know.

Clearly, a very careful line has to be drawn.

This posture, one of subordination to the task, and a genuine desire to understand not only the job, but also the pressures and circumstances under which the other party has to work, means that the writer must leave his ego at the door. Any knowledge he or she has of the task, or any previous intelligence about how the subject is likely to react, is of little consequence to the task in hand. The writer's job is to learn - quickly, accurately, and with a real respect for what the user of the system has to do. If this is not taken on board properly, the most horrendous and inappropriate solutions to the documentation requirement will result.

This is not to say that the interview need not include little titbits that will interest the user and even get them just a little bit excited about what is to come. In a very real sense, good documentation is welcomed by an anxious public, particularly when a new system is being introduced. Part of the writer's job is to herald the arrival of the new documentation in an enthusiastic and positive way.

Therefore, to the ability to write, we must add very sensitive investigative skills. We must also mix in a sense of humour, confidence without boorish certainty, attention to detail, and a willingness to ask questions again and again until there is no possibility of misunderstanding.

The last skill that a writer must bring to the party is an ability to see how complex ideas could be explained by the use of diagrams. 'Not a problem,' you say, 'we have our own graphic designer.' Well, lucky old you - but it is still what you call a 'problem'. The graphic designer may be hugely competent at his or her craft, but mind-reading is unlikely to be a part of their skill set. The designer will not take part in the interviews and surveys and will not, therefore, get a real handle on the job you hope to document. It is, therefore, imperative that the writer thinks about diagrammatic interpretations of the task from the outset.

In very many organisations the writer is also the illustrator and thought about diagrams at the outset will do much to help in the writing task and may do much to enhance the reputation of the writer in their organisation.

If you think that you have these many and varied qualities, you may have the makings of a good technical author. Alternatively, you may know of someone else who fits the bill. The rest of the chapters in this book will explain how you or your colleague can build on these capabilities, sharpen up your skills, and apply your talents to the writing, design, and publishing of user manuals.

3 Investigation - the key to a good result

In this chapter we will discuss the need for an investigative process that takes the practical requirements of the user into consideration. Much of what needs to be said, both here and later in the book, can be expressed most clearly by reference to an example. Here and in succeeding chapters, we use a fictional company taking telephone orders for the despatch of goods as our example. More of this later in the chapter.

3.1 The investigation stages

There are two stages of investigation in the writing process. The aim in the initial one is to develop ideas about the documentation requirements, leading to the production of an outline of the book or books required. This outline is known as a synopsis and is described in more detail in Chapter 5. In order to prepare a good synopsis, you have to know something of the readership's job, education, and inclination to read. You also have to know more than a little concerning the topic to be written about - be it a stock controller's manual, a credit controller's handbook, a set of standards and procedures governing security and backup practices in a large mainframe computer suite, or a large system encompassing all these elements and many more.

The second investigative stage is where you need to go into the subject in greater depth and emerge with sufficient detail to write the books. Depending on the system and your situation, you may already have done much of this research at the earlier stage, but there will, undoubtedly, be areas where you feel less than comfortable about the information gained previously.

So how much do you really know about the topic or the audience? To start work with little knowledge of the latter would constitute a mortal sin, but it is possible to gain the former as you go along. We will start with a look at that most critical area - your audience.

3.2   Considering your audience

I am afraid that I may have done the creative writer a disservice in the Preface to this book.

I implied that all a novelist needs to do is to conjure up a good story-line and then let rip on the typewriter. This, of course, is not the whole story, but those of us who earn our living from a more fundamental branch of the art form may learn something from the element that I conveniently omitted.

Even the best novelists must write for the market - or at least they must do so if they want to be published. They must, therefore, shape their imagination and their creativity into one of two planes. They must either write for the popular market, which means that title style, length, subject matter, and targeted audience will all be dictated before the first sheet of paper is wound into the Remington, or they must write something that strikes out into uncharted territory, but which is both well written and somehow 'catches the moment'. Take, as recent examples, Shirley Conran or the Collins sisters for the former and Joseph Heller (*Catch-22*) for the latter.

Now, if it is right that creative writers satisfy the needs of their audience, how much more true this must be for the writer of user guides.

Consequently, I would suggest that, before spending any time thinking about the product or service that is to be the subject of the documentation, the professional writer of user guides should investigate the audience in detail. After all, the subtitle of this book is *A practical guide for those who want to be read* and unless the audience is understood, this objective is unlikely to be satisfied.

'User' is a term that has, in computer circles, achieved a derogatory taint to it. In a sense it has had to, because the trend towards packaged software solutions relies upon diminishing the importance of user satisfaction. Standard user interfaces, standard products, standard predetermined system results - all may reduce costs for the software user and increase profits for the software supplier, but there is a price to be paid. This is the imposition of solutions upon the user family, who, as a consequence, must either relearn their tasks within the context of the standard solution or carry on working in the old way and add the skill of subliminal interpreter to their job description.

This to my mind unsatisfactory situation may in time swing the other way again. I say 'again' because the earliest days of commercial data processing would not have come about had such a high-handed attitude been peddled by the computer industry. Those old enough to remember the heady days of tabulators, plugged-program computers, and the mag-striped card wonders of NCR and Burroughs will remember the inordinate lengths systems engineers went to to mimic the status quo.

Perhaps there will be a 21st century version of the Peasants' Revolt (there I go by careless talk falling into the derogatory trap!) which will unite users and their managements in a movement that says 'bespoke yes, off the peg, no', but until that day there will be a gulf between the precise needs of the user family and what their managements are prepared to buy.

This breach can, in part, be filled by good documentation. A good explanation can provide a user with the information he or she needs in order to see their job in the context of the computer system, and do much, as a consequence, to reduce the time taken for systems absorption. To some extent this may be called 'sympathy writing', in that sympathy, while it does not solve a problem, does make the recipient of the sympathy at least feel better!

If you accept this premise, you must agree that few existing user guides pass muster. How many user guides that you have read recently adopt a posture which has as its underlying message, 'Come on, let's get together and make the best of things'. Not that documentation should be apologetic - far from it, but there is a case for a little humility and understanding - sympathy, if you like.

Even a product or service that is not packaged is likely to be something of a compromise to many members of the user family. Somewhere along the line during the design process, arbitrary decisions will have been made and commercial objectives will have taken precedence over individual need. To keep a sense of balance, we must not ignore the fact that, just occasionally, users' requests can be quite cranky! Here, too, documentation can be used to win the hearts and minds of anxious potential users, but only where the writer is prepared to put a lot of time and effort into getting to know the readership in terms of its attitude, motivation, and business function.

I use the word 'anxious' intentionally. Users are universally anxious. Whatever their station in life, they suffer to a greater or lesser degree from technoanxiety. This condition has many symptoms. Watching executives, who are not associated with an IT department, using a computer terminal is rather like studying children riding donkeys on a beach. Some are confident and matter-of-fact about the whole business, while others are, by turns, nervous, petrified, and rather embarrassed - the last category trying vainly to will the whole ghastly business to end as quickly as possible, while scanning sea and landscape in a vain effort to avoid eye contact with sundry doting relatives watching from the safety of terra firma.

In the office environment, substitute colleagues for the doting relatives.

The management suites of big companies even today are filled with people who are only too happy to lean proprietorially over their screens when they are switched off, but who will exude the scent of fear if they have to use the wretched things for anything other than interrogating their diaries or drafting an internal memo. Few feel happy even signing on to their terminals and some do not even know what that phrase means.

Lack of use at management level often means that buying decisions for computer systems are based solely on the functions that can be provided without reference to the ease of use, quality of documentation, or any other in-depth thought about the needs of the day-to-day users.

This, ultimately, has an effect on the way that the system is used once it is installed. Training, when provided, tends to concentrate on actual system use and users are rarely treated to an overall picture of the system, seeing where their particular cog fits into the overall pattern. In addition, a general fear of technology and the use of unfriendly 'jargon' words on computer menus means that people are reluctant to delve into the system and find out about the extra features it can offer. Therefore many people use the equipment and software available to them on a very basic level - only able to perform tasks associated with the mainstream of their job within the organisation. This means that most, if not all, of the fancy little features that represent the buying triggers resulting in the installation of the system in the first place are ignored by the user population.

Furthermore, many more users are unable to interpret the results presented to them by the system. Reports and enquiries are often ignored, and the 'scoring' of the day-to-day operation of the system is left to the computer literate - at whatever level in the organisation.

To sum up the argument so far, the shortfall between reality and the perfect world can be explained by a fear of technology, a lack of comprehensive systems understanding, a lack of interpretive skills, and the fact that most systems do not do (for whatever reason) exactly what the users either want or expect.

But 'users' is not only a tainted, derogatory term. It is also a generalisation - a collective noun that masks individuality. It smacks of a sort of benign racism, heralding in a sort of humour that some find deeply offensive and even sinister. 'We would be all right if it weren't for the users', is a common complaint in the computer department.

Fair enough. At one level, it is faintly funny, a sort of safety valve much released on the help desk. But it is also an outrage. Without users there would be no computers, no careers, no help desks. Users are king. They can make or break a computer system. And they are all different. From the author's point of view, even the scoffing computer technician is, in his particular calling, a user. Many of the best arguments for the preparation of user documentation by professional writers are to be found in the fringes of the computer department. Many mistakes are made by those who 'run' computer systems on behalf of the more obvious departmental applications users - mistakes that can be reduced or eliminated by the availability of good 'user-orientated' documentation.

The author, having taken on board the shortcomings of the systems and the anxieties of the audience described at length above, has this other major consideration to address, namely the infinite variety of vocations that constitutes the user family. Some are computer literate and confident, the success stories on those beach donkeys. Some are lacking in confidence - or just plain uninterested. Some need to know how to interpret the information on the computer, while others must simply undertake a routine task quickly and efficiently. Some are concerned with setting up and maintaining the system data, while others merely use it. Some are only concerned with the management of the system - the switching on and off, the backing up and restoring, the upkeep of the passwords and user access profiles. Some are meant to train potential users, while others are intended to support actual users.

If we again look at our illustration (Figure 3.1) of the flow of information in the company, we can see the types of staff using the system at each level.

Figure 3.1
Computer system users

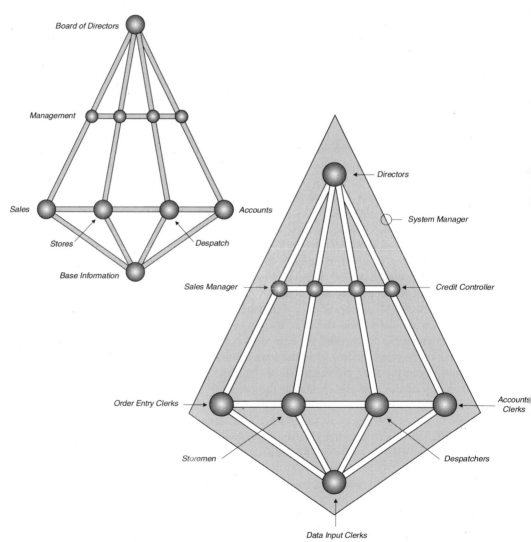

Who, understanding the realities of how a computer system really works in an organisation, could then recommend the preparation of a total, all-embracing, system user guide - a single volume describing the process? It would be like giving every member of a symphony orchestra the conductor's score. Only the conductor needs to know what everyone is doing - he is the symphonic help desk, and a 'combined volume' has a role to play in the commercial auditorium as well. But percussion, first violins, flutes, credit controllers, stock controllers, order entry clerks, directors - all need a separate document - pitched (sorry!) at their level and containing the information that they require to undertake their task to the good of the whole activity.

3.3   Determining the optimum length of the books

Short books are more likely to be read than long ones. It is also true to say that righteous indignation on the part of writer or management is more justified over an unread book of 5,000 words - say 30 pages, than 80,000 words or 480 pages. More importantly, the short book will not only be read, it will be understood - providing, of course, that it is well written.

It should be clear that the writer, if he or she follows this line of argument, is, at this stage, extremely busy trying to sift through a welter of data that has not yet really touched upon the subject matter of the system or service in question at all. The detail of the stock control system, accounting system, or procedure being documented, is not yet under investigation and it will never supersede the central issue of the users' requirements in the writer's thoughts.

The first priority is to know the audience and what they want to achieve, and appreciate the shortcomings of the subject matter in the eyes of that audience. From this will stem a realisation that most systems are wholly used by nobody - save the help desk - and there is a golden opportunity to provide brief books that will be more readily understood by the readership if their manual is restricted to what they have to know, plus a succinct overview that sets their task into the context of the whole system.

So you are going to write short books that address the audience and, to some extent, the task. By this last comment, I infer that we may treat setting up the system, installing the system, and supporting the system in a technical sense as quite discrete from day-to-day running in all the relevant departments of the company.

It may still take 80,000 words to describe a complex system, so the work of the writer is not drastically curtailed. The important thing is a recognition that many short volumes are infinitely better than one big tome. Of course, this means that the writer must be so much more than a mere scribe.

He has to research, to understand, to sympathise, and to solve a very tricky problem - the dissemination of information in a totally new 'mix' that will require, if the job is to be done properly, a modest helping of lateral thinking.

And we still know little or nothing about the system that is to be described.

But, we have radically altered what we will eventually write. Why? Because, having decided to write books to satisfy departmental aspirations, it is difficult to see why we ever considered writing books based on system structure. The old approach of marching through the menus laboriously - main menu, then each of the sub-menus - is entirely inappropriate to a book that will be read by, say, the order processing clerk.

3.4   Looking at the system

The writer must, of necessity, tackle the system from two angles. It is necessary to examine not only the 'nuts and bolts' of the system structure, options, and features, but also the practical application of each element.

Let us take our example routine of telephone order processing. Now, as everybody knows, order processing is normally about matching customer requirements to catalogue items and then ensuring that the items are sourced, despatched, and then, either as part of the order processing element or in a discrete sub-module, invoiced. From that point invoice details go on to the ledgers.

There is, of course, a world of difference between order processing in a telephone-sales, mail-order company, and order processing at an antique shop. The principles are the same, but one is high volume where customer satisfaction is measured by speed, efficiency, and being convinced that your order has been taken correctly, and the other is all about customer service - taking time and going to extreme lengths over delivery details.

Let us examine in detail the documentation of a sales order processing system in a telephone-sales, mail-order company, as this is the more likely of the two to be the subject of a professional documentation exercise.

The computer system to reflect such an activity might include the following modules:

- stock control, including provision for back-orders
- customer credit checking
- credit card details processing
- order processing, including interface with the stock, customer credit, and credit card modules
- despatch planning, including details of expected arrival at the customer's premises
- preparation of picking and despatch documentation

- despatch confirmation and invoice production
- sales and commission analysis - be they by product, sales area, representative, advertising medium (catalogue, television or newspaper advertisement, etc.), or telesales operative, or a combination of elements
- accounting systems, particularly the purchase and nominal ledgers.

It will be seen from this that what appears to be a straightforward process is, in fact, rather complex. The computer system to reflect a telesales operation has, above all, to be very fast indeed. A number of disparate systems - stock control, order processing, despatch, the processing of payment details, even manufacturing - must all be consulted within the few moments available to the telesales operative. If they are not, the operative must ad lib, to the intense annoyance of the customer.

Everyone has had experiences where telephone ordering has gone like a dream - ordering concert or theatre tickets seems to be particularly successful - and others where a gloomy sense of foreboding seems to take over as the telephone handset is returned to its cradle. Did they get the catalogue number right? He didn't repeat it to me. I *did* say the 22.30 sleeper from Euston to Inverness, didn't I? And what was the date?

Seen from the computer's point of view, such an exercise involves the interrogation of several quite separate systems of mind boggling complexity. Taking just the stock system as an example, the following information might be required to be able to conduct an accurate assessment of availability:

- product codes, descriptions, prices, margins, sources of supply, quantities available, quantities on order, quantities already allocated to customers willing to wait on an extended delivery, expected delivery times, substitute products (if any), details of product termination, price rises - together with dates, packing details, etc., for every line.

The effect of interrogating the files and actually placing an order will result in significant changes to the files and generate a need for reaction on the part of the computer system:

- order acceptance will result in the updating of this information in real time, and the allocation of stock through the despatch system for delivery.
- satisfying the stock/order processing element will be mechanisms for applying new stock to the system as it is delivered. This will include matching deliveries against orders, checking quality, coping with rejection due to damage, etc., discrepancies between order and sales measure (ordered in dozens, hundreds, tonnes - sold in units, etc.), the allocation of stock to certain warehouses and bays within those warehouses. This will be affected by the nature of the goods in question - for example, you would be unlikely to keep lawnmowers and food hampers on the same shelves.

Behind stock delivery and despatch are the supporting accounting processes and ordering systems based on past sales performance and sales projections. The latter will be affected by promotions and seasonal factors (barbecues in summer, antifreeze in winter, etc.).

It would be job enough to document the system for stock accurately and many authors would see this as their task and would feel that they had done rather well if after several months of studying the systems or functional specifications and talking to the software people they gave birth to a wordy tome entitled *Stock Control*.

But who would use such an undoubtedly long book? Once again, we have to refer back to our audience. The stock system is used by accountants, buyers, despatchers, marketing people, territory sales staff, directors, warehousemen, and telesales staff. How would they know where to look in this large document for an answer to their particular problem?

If you accept the approach of writing for the audience, you must accept the need for user documentation for all of the groups of employees mentioned above. But not restricted to the stock system, for none of their jobs is limited to the activities found in the stock module of the computer system alone.

The accountant will see the achievement of good margins and the successful implementation of just-in-time techniques to keep unsold stocks held to a minimum as a very small, if, nonetheless, important part of his job.

The telesales staff are only interested in the stock situation insofar as it affects them. In other words, the stock recording must be accurate, and the system must be easy to operate. Their job, however, like those undertaken by all the other people in our scenario, cuts across systems demarcation lines and to document the system in terms of computer routine is to miss out on a vital point.

Look at the telesales person's job for just a minute. They must, first of all, be very alert and have a good telephone manner. The public, telephoning an order for a compilation record, a set of pans, or a patent fluff remover, will tolerate a minimum of questions and delay and will expect courtesy and clarity from the sales person. When the public ring off, they want to feel confident that their order is going to be swiftly and efficiently executed.

The telesales person has three things to help them - their own steady nerves, a good telephone device, and a first-class computer system. When the phone rings, the telesales person answers and asks what they may do to help. As they are talking, they are accessing the Order Entry module of the system. Joe Public mumbles that they want something, usually by giving the name of the item. The telesales person tries to encourage the customer to quote the product number. This results in accessing the Stock system, first for confirmation of the product - quoting the full description in order to confirm any catalogue number provided by the potential buyer - and, of course, to make sure that both parties are talking about the same item. There may then be a need to further refine the order ('was that the pink or the blue you wanted Madam?'). Once the number required has been ascertained, the order processing module must check the stocks to confirm the fact that the item is in stock.

If the item is available, or the customer is willing to wait until delivery to the warehouse takes place, it is then over to the despatch area of the system to confirm the date of delivery in 'your part of the country' (if it is done by 'own vehicle').

Once this is clarified, it is over to the customer credit checking part of the system. 'Have you dealt with us before, and, if so, are you able to quote your existing customer number?' From here, we drift into credit card systems - blacklists as soon as the 4929 number is quoted - and then on to expiry dates for further checking purposes.

Once all is satisfied, the order is displayed on the screen for a final verbal confirmation. 'No. 1234, The Toaster in blue, price £49.95, your credit card number 4929 751 684 412, Mrs. Padlock, of 2, Cold Street, Tumuli-on-Humber, South Humberside, Postcode DN29 5IW. Delivery will be next Thursday by our vehicle between 9.00 a.m. and 12.30 p.m. Thank you very much for your order'... and on to the next one.

Such pressured people as telesales staff hardly need a stock system manual, accompanied by other manuals for all the other systems they are using. They barely need a book at all, but if they do have one - or perhaps some kind of a quick reference card - it should be about order processing as they do it and as it has been described above.

This demonstrates graphically how a good writer is not going to take the easy way out of writing voluminous books reflecting the computer systems determined by programmers and analysts alike. Rather, he or she will spend some time with each of the working groups. He or she is not only concerned with the job and system specifications but also with how those are translated into blood, sweat, and labour in the office or workplace. Just what does each job entail in terms of activity, volume, and pressure? Clearly, our telesales person seems to have a simple and routine task of perhaps two minute's duration, repeated over and over again throughout the working day. However, the circumstances of their work puts them under enormous pressure as they need speed, precision, accuracy, and good manners. As a consequence, in terms of support, they need nothing more than a good *aide memoire* for the odd 'funny' that they will sometimes have to handle. Training, and a short training manual, should do the rest.

Although this chapter is about investigation in general, you can once again see the need to study the audience in great detail. The system can only truly be examined in the context of the way in which it is used. Think about the conclusions drawn above concerning the nature of the telephone salespersons' work. Such an understanding can only come from sitting and watching the operatives going about their daily duties. The writer would, however, be strongly advised to spend some time also with their supervisor, and to see how middle management view the work and encourage productivity.

A superficial visit to a sales office may leave one with a lasting impression of ringing telephones, clattering keyboards, and structured telephone conversations. But, what else may you draw from the visit? Is the computer system truly operating in real-time, or is there an element of catching up to do when the customer rings off? A surprising number of on-line, real-time systems simply cannot keep up, and when the customer rings off, the telephone sales operative is left typing in some of the details - either from memory or a much-thumbed reporter's notebook.

Is the sales operative also responsible for managing a printer? Once again, many order processing jobs involve tearing off combined order dockets and picking notes and then depositing these in baskets for collection in batches. A user document concentrating on the true order processing element but ignoring the output would be of little value in this example - but you might overlook it, and this error of omission in your synopsis and maybe your book may lead the reviewer to a conclusion about your work as a whole that is far from accurate.

Lastly, does the supervisor set competitions for numbers of orders, value, tonnage, new customers signed, etc.? Does this throw the frenetic but ordered routine of the office into complete turmoil - and make work quality suffer as a result?

Such intelligence about the audience and the way in which they relate to the system will have a marked effect on the type of book the sensitive writer will write and, clearly, to sit down and write the book without a very clear understanding of how it might be read would be extremely irresponsible. It might even be the case that on-line help, very carefully written of course, would be more appropriate than even a quick reference card. Such recommendations and the preparation of the text for on-line help are also an author's legitimate task.

While the processes described above will also be undertaken in our antique shop, the need for lightening-speed support will not be a factor. That being the case, any software house developing a speculative software product for the antiques trade would be well within their rights to develop a task-driven user guide that took time to inform and explain what has to be done - and why.

Similar processes, therefore, may have vastly different solutions - depending upon the circumstances under which they are operated.

3.5   Starting the investigation

Clearly, if you are to write a book for someone whose job it is to enter order details, we must write a book that is task driven, not system driven. You must look through the telescope from the other end - seeing the computer system in the context of the commercial objective, rather than disregarding everything that is not concerned with fields, screens, and menu options.

This, of course, greatly adds to the writer's task. To your appreciation of the fact that you must fill the gap between aspiration and reality and understand the fears of your audience, you must now become fully cognisant with the workings of every department likely to use the system. But part of this work is already done. If the audience can be identified fragmentally, each task can be investigated individually and the knowledge of the system will fall out of an effective departmental investigation. Very rapidly, your version of the Information CAGE will develop in your mind.

In this book we have assumed that the writer is in the ideal position of having actual or potential system users to interview. If the writer is not in this fortunate situation, he will have to try to glean the information in other ways. For example, the writer could speak to the analysts who designed the system or to other people inside or outside the organisation who have experience of the business area concerned.

Given that you do have access to users, the normal method of investigation is to carry out a series of interviews with departmental staff to ascertain their working practices. 'What do you do? What do you need to know to carry out your work effectively? What must you hand on to the next department(s) in the process?', are all common questions. The reaction on the part of the interviewee is usually very positive, but this can result in the outpouring of a great deal of emotion and prejudice which, although interesting for the amateur psychiatrist, leaves the writer trying hard to fathom where this all fits into the grand plan of the computer system.

If the computer system is already installed and running, whether in a live or test environment, the writer will also need to ask questions about how they use various elements of the system and try to fit this information into the overall impression gained.

The outcome of the interview can also, in extreme cases, be very dangerous. It is sometimes clear that these basic questions were never asked by the systems analyst whose job it was to specify the computer system or take part in the selection process from the various packages on the market. Alternatively, the questions may have been asked, but requirements in other areas have taken precedence over those of the individual facing the writer. If this conclusion is drawn, the gap between aspiration and reality may be disappointingly wide and some head-scratching and politicking may ensue.

However, I maintain that the writer's 'boss', is the audience and writer effectiveness must be measured by the eventual universal acceptance of the system. Writers' success is also about accurate interpretation of the results obtained by the system on the part of the management, accurate use by those who 'feed' the system, and the speedy implementation of new and updated versions of the system. The writers' work can save many times the cost of their employment, but only if their contribution is accurately measured, and this may mean cutting through the politics of an organisation.

Perhaps this is one advantage the contract writer has over the full-time employee. It is easier to be true to one's ideals when constrained only by the commercial realities of the next contract, when the alternative might be a stained reputation on an otherwise upwardly mobile member of the organisation.

3.6   Determining the book titles and types

Gradually, each departmental investigation will allow the writer to start to see the menu options in terms of the commercial objectives. The degree of complete or partial overlap may be significant. For example, almost anyone may want to make an enquiry on a customer or supplier name and address, a currency code, or a stock item. Partial overlap occurs where the programmer has combined different tasks departmentally into one convenient (to him) program or menu option. Customer records are often used by the sales team (territory code), order processing department (customer number for verification purposes), credit controller (credit limits and rolling current indebtedness), despatch (delivery details), and general accounts (name and address for invoicing purposes). All one option from the computer programmer's point of view - add, maintain, view a customer - but used in different ways and never wholly by any one department.

The writer must not, of course, refer the user to another book which happens to contain the definitive information about the customer record. If he is writing for the user, he cannot fall into the trap already occupied by the programmer. The information must be repeated in the case of complete overlap or the 'Gospel according to ...' of the New Testament must be the role model in the case of partial overlap.

So, referring to the Information CAGE superimposed by the book titles (see Figure 3.2), we see that the books required must closely match the departmental and management structure. In addition, as individual departments may draw information from the central files, so the books for those departments need to show how this is done.

3.7   Avoiding the pitfalls

We haven't even looked at the sensitive area of the readers' willingness to read the books - yet.

Perhaps it is time to tackle this thorny area. After all, the technical or business author's objective is to transfer his acquired knowledge and understanding into the users' heads, so that they can undertake their work with accuracy and a degree of willingness and enthusiasm born out of feeling comfortable about their work. But, can you as the writer know how often your audience - depending on the book being written - reads books at all? And if they do read, would they read your manual out of choice?

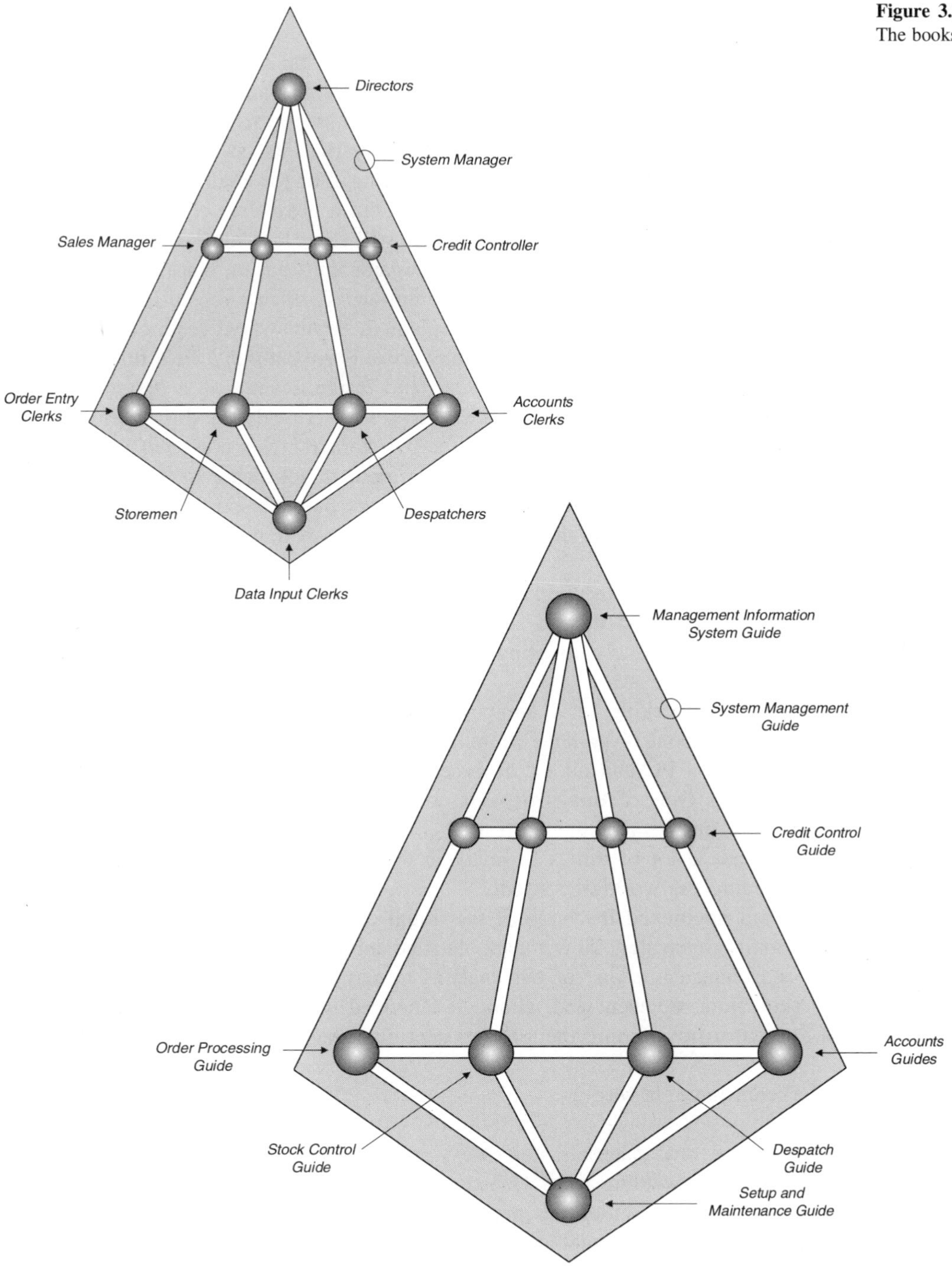

Figure 3.2
The books the users need

It is not the professional writer's job to proselytise in favour of the merits of reading. Furthermore, a book cannot legislate for itself being read. It does not have the authority of a senior manager breathing down the neck of an unfortunate recruit. It does not even have the authority of the tutor on a training course who can demand to be listened to, even when he is indescribably boring. It has no more authority than its cover design and its attractiveness to the audience in terms of being 'not too long' or being 'easy to use'. Little or no authority at all, in fact, but a great deal of responsibility. As we said earlier, even the willing reader will soon lose interest if he or she finds errors of fact or omission. The investigator must ensure that the true facts emerge - not just users' wish lists or assumptions. Furthermore, sufficient detail must emerge to allow the writer to explain in depth, where required, and to clear up any misunderstandings that may arise. For example, a field titled 'PT' on the customer record may look small and insignificant, but if it stands for 'payment terms', the default being 30 days, it is critical that this is changed at the time of input for potentially bad customers who must pay cash on delivery. If the person responsible for this input is not aware of this, it could lead to the company accepting some unnecessary bad debts. After all, how can the delivery driver know that he has to collect cash if it does not appear on the delivery docket?

So don't skimp on the research. Watch your audience at work - not in the manner of a time and motion study expert. This means no clipboards please! Nothing is more likely to bring a workplace to a complete standstill. An exaggeration? Not at all.

I was once working for a computer supplier that specialised in the supply of production control systems running on what were called minis. They had the power of a PC and all the elegance of an army surplus tin desk, but we loved them. One of our prospects was an engineering company in the automotive business in the north-west of England. It was the seventies, so Britain made a lot of things in metal in those days, but also had a high old time keeping the workforce sweet.

We had negotiated the hoop of the initial call and the production manager was looking interested. Now for the detailed survey. I was the salesman on the call and along came one of our analysts to carry out the survey. Down onto the shop floor we went and, although I noticed the clipboard, I didn't see it as a threat to my joining the 100 per cent club that year.

I should have. It was.

Down to the raw materials store we went and looked knowledgeably at the steel coils and welding rods. Questions were asked. The pencil moved. The clipboard groaned under the pressure of the constantly turning page. My production manager contact started to go a little pale and ran, in a rather undignified way, to a wall-mounted phone. As we made our way out of the raw materials store and into the first production area - a sheet metal guillotine shop - unknown to us, our visit was, in strange parallel to the life of Marie Antoinette, rapidly drawing to a close.

Things then happened very quickly indeed. An immaculately dressed individual whom I had not noticed before came sweeping up the shop floor with an entourage which included a rather shamefaced man who had, until a moment ago, been talking to us in the raw materials store. Mr Smart was not interested in us, but took the hapless production manager aside. There was never any doubt that we were what we said we were, but consultations had not taken place, a precedent had been set, and face had been lost.

Retribution was swift.

It is only when the noise of a busy factory stops that you realise just how noisy they are. Nothing but a few conversations and the sound of a lone apprentice whistling out of tune as he made his way over to a singing kettle. We left rather quickly, never to return. After an hour or so, we had it on good authority, the factory started work again but we had unwittingly blotted the production manager's copy book and I was *persona non grata* for it.

So, remember that you are the friend of your audience and not their enemy. If your book is intended to encourage, support, assist, and generate enthusiasm, then so must your behaviour during the survey stage.

3.8   Summary

It can be seen from this investigative approach that an understanding of the system comes, not from endless poring over a screen or study of the systems specifications - valuable though these are - but from a gradual piecing together of the system from the users' practical explanation of what they do. It is rather like taking a complicated meal and, by the employment of intricate analytical skills, working out the ingredients and quantities that were used in order to develop the recipe.

One trick when carrying out an investigation is to think of each department as requiring answers to a series of questions. This is a good discipline, as it provides a framework for the writing task, while at the same time providing a blueprint from which the user can work when performing the all-important task of reviewing the synopsis. This will be discussed later in this book.

4 Paper based or electronic - the pros and cons of modern technology and the development of on-line manuals

One of the things now available that was not around in my early days is the concept of electronic support for the end-user. This support can be provided at a variety of levels, from fairly straightforward on-line help through to the use of hypertext, which provides almost limitless hierarchies of advice to satisfy any level of enquiry.

Indeed, it is also now possible to integrate systems with computer-based training (CBT) methods, so that the user can break off in the middle of a job and work through an example that is related to the topic of their memory lapse.

So, how should we be producing our documents? Should we be sticking to the old, familiar, paper-based format, or should we be taking advantage of the new technology available to us?

This chapter discusses some of this technology and provides you with some pointers to help you decide whether you can take advantage of its features, or whether a hard-copy book still provides the best solution for your situation.

4.1 How we read books and why

Some believed that the advent of on-line text would sound the death knell of the user guide in its conventional 'black ink on white paper' manifestation. After all, we are, we are told, living in the age of the paperless office. Why not get the technology to help out if it can do so? Besides, what about the rain forests?

Despite all the compelling arguments, this transition has not happened yet, although the trend is now moving more quickly in that direction. I believe that there are several very good arguments for this apparent example of latter-day Luddism.

First, let us absolve the writers of any bias. We should have no axe to grind. If our skill is in writing - explaining complex processes through the medium of the written word - there is as much of a career for us in the preparation of words on screen as there is on paper. This is not to say that additional skills may not be invaluable or even essential. Some may argue that to build successful on-line documentation dialogue design must be understood thoroughly. These skills may be acquired directly or through collusion with others. However, the underlying principles which the writer must address remain the same.

As always, we must start with the ultimate user of the documentation. In order that you make the right choice of documentation medium, it is important to understand how people read documentation and why they might, for preference, choose one medium rather than another.

Study of the way we read shows that the screen is rather unforgiving. Watch anyone reading a book and it is very likely that you will see a manifestation of a strange phenomenon every time, or at least most times, the foot of a page is reached.

Studies show that we, in fact, read at up to three positions on the page. We read ahead of ourselves, read at the correct linear position, and read at the back - picking up on any last-minute points. This is not observable until the bottom of a page is reached in a tranche of text that continues indefinitely. However, when the ideas and the text go on over the page, the reader will often be observed to flick the page back and forth until those three stages of reading have lodged the ideas firmly in the reader's mind and progress is assured.

Clearly a book is an ideal medium to satisfy this requirement. It is very easy to manipulate and highly mechanical. You can put your finger on the line you have reached when you are interrupted. You can even 'dog' the page when it is time to call it a day.

Life is not so easy with screen-based documents. For a start, unless you are fortunate enough to have access to a large screen, restrictions on screen size mean that a screen-based 'page' is vastly smaller than its hard-copy rival (accommodating about as much information as a single page in a *Mr. Men* book). Although marking facilities emulating the finger on the page and the bookmark are available in a number of on-line documentation products, it is still not possible to flick backwards and forwards in the same way as one does with a book. Scrolling down through the text inevitably means that earlier sections disappear from the screen. Yes, I know it is quite easy to press the Page-up key, or use your mouse to scroll backwards, to go back to 'catch up', but most people don't. For them, what happens is a sort of distanced lazy reading where the sense of the text is not really 'going in'. But they read on, nevertheless. At the end of the exercise, the brain makes a sort of judgement about what to do, based on what it has accumulated in the way of information. There is little doubt that in this instance what it has accumulated will be sketchy compared with the more accessible and more familiar hard-copy version.

Many people display a conscious recognition of this problem and will only be happy if they can see hard-copy text displayed before them. For these people, if documentation is provided on-line, it is unlikely to be used well unless the facility is also provided to print the details out. It is important to remember that even if you feel happy with reading text on a screen and absorb it well, you cannot assume that others feel the same. Fortunately, the ability to print is an option with most, if not all, on-line documentation systems. However, you must remember that, unless the product you are using has the ability to print text in different formats, the text will have been formatted for viewing on-line and may not be such an easy read when seen on paper.

People may also prefer books for purely psychological reasons. If a user makes a mistake with their computer system, they suffer from a cocktail of emotions. They feel inadequate, embarrassed, and annoyed with themselves and the system. They may not feel confident enough to search on the system for further information. Indeed, if the problem appears to come from the system itself, they may not have much faith in doing so. At times like these, it is comforting to turn to a lifeline that is familiar. We all know the feel, the weight, and the workings of a book. Providing the information is there and the way to it is well signposted, a hard-copy manual has an inside track over the screen-based support provided.

You should also remember, particularly where matters of policy, standards, or procedure are concerned, that the printed word has more authority than that on the screen. This is by virtue of the feeling of 'ownership' that the reader has for a book, something not possible for text on the screen.

Another reason for the continuance of the printed word is tied into one of the underlying principles that this book subscribes to. User documentation, we think, should be driven by user need. It should reflect the commercial tasks rather than the computer system. It should be possible for the user to understand how to achieve his commercial objective before he even switches his terminal on. Many commercial activities travel across computer system options in an amazing tracery that is as complex as the Underground map over the face of London. Support that is tied to the pressing of the Help key from a system option cannot hope to identify the ultimate objective of every user and offer appropriate advice.

Furthermore, users will often wish to take a book away from the office to mull over on a train or over a cup of coffee, to think about the system and try to gain some understanding of it away from the busy office environment. Although this may be possible with portable technology, it is not always practical. Some hypertext systems allow you to insert your own annotations, explanations, and bookmarks, but can high technology really compete with the pencilled aside, the highlighter pen, or the yellow sticker?

Finally, there is one essential thing that you can do with a book that is simply not possible with on-line text - you can flick through it. In the final event, when all attempts at searching via contents lists and indices have failed, a quick flick through a book may allow you to catch a glimpse of the item you are looking for and help you locate it.

All this is not to say that you should not use on-line text at all - in fact, quite the contrary, as the final section in this chapter indicates. You must, however, as with other aspects of document production, take the needs of the user into consideration, and determine when and where on-line or hard-copy solutions are more appropriate.

4.2   A brief history of on-line text

Initially, help text was only available in error situations where it was siamese-twinned to the screen and interface program code. This made it practically impossible for the text to be written by anyone other than the programmer. Just as programmers used not to be noted for their sartorial elegance, nor were they particularly remembered for their precise and down-to-earth explanations - orally, or in writing. Nor, indeed, did they always have a full understanding of the impact that items they considered to be trivial could have on their poor unsuspecting users. Even today, a programmer is most valuable when his or her strongest affinity is with the machine and its operating environment and the development tools.

This did not do good things for hard-coded on-line text. I well remember an otherwise very professional little software house that had reams of on-line text supporting a software product running on a mid-range system. The error help was provided in the form of a code number which appeared on the screen along with standard supporting text. The worst possible message, heralded with a sense of the theatrical by the code '99', was defined as 'catastrophic error - no help available'. As this was one of seventy or so error messages, it did not really stand out when it appeared in a list. Even so, the message had an apocalyptic ring to it.

Unfortunately, the programmers in this organisation were a tidy-minded bunch and, aware of the need for error messages that actually worked, in went 99 as a 'catchall' - a sort of software curbstone in the cul-de-sac of every program. If nothing else was provided as a warning in the case of wrongful use, up would flash error message 99. As with most computer systems, coding was performed under a certain amount of pressure and there was simply no time to sort out the error messages. Consequently, finger-trouble, letters in numeric fields, the date inserted in the wrong format - all resulted in the display of the digital grim reaper and his message of terrifying damnation. I never did find out if they corrected this before the system was delivered to an unsuspecting client.

Although things have clearly moved on from those times, this anecdote does serve to illustrate the point that text to be available on-line must be applied judiciously, and its positioning and structure deserve every bit as much consideration as do the book titles and structure for books.

Nowadays, electronic help has a much wider application than simply error messages. The text itself is more easily maintained, and is usually provided in separate text files which contain 'hooks' into the software at appropriate places and levels. Thus, a simple sign-on screen may have support provided at screen level, whereas a more complex screen will require - and have - support at field level. Of course, even technology-shy authors can quickly learn to provide text on this basis and, all things being equal, a greater level of clarity and precision can be obtained.

Until the recent advent of windows-type products, the ergonomics of on-line support were rather poor. In most cases on-screen help entirely replaced what was formerly on the screen. So, you had a problem and decided to resort to the help screen. Fortunately, help was there and it explained in great detail what you wanted to know. However, what you were working on was, of course, no longer on the screen, so you tried to memorise the advice and then return to your working screen.

Just at the critical moment the phone rang or some kindly soul asked you if you would like a cup of coffee. When you returned to your work you had not only forgotten the advice but also the problem you had in the first place. So after answering the phone and acknowledging the kind offer of a cuppa, you had to start again. In all that fiasco, you would have been much better off with a book you could have referred to while the screen upon which you were having a problem was still on view with the cursor conveniently marking the problem area.

The advent of windows-type products, allowing you to view help alongside your working screen, has alleviated this problem for many systems, but it continues to be present for users of mid-range and mainframe systems with traditional terminals. As windows-type products become more and more widely available, the ergonomics problem of on-line text will largely disappear.

Similarly, until recently, help was restricted to the provision of simple character-based text. Diagrams could only be included providing they could be drawn using standard keyboard characters. Once again, for some mid-range and mainframe systems this is still very much the case. However, in other areas this aspect has improved greatly.

With developments in the area of hypertext, things have now advanced to a more complex level. On-line support now allows you to enquire in a number of directions from your starting point, delving ever deeper into the information provided in an endeavour to find the relevant detail. The ability to include detailed diagrams and iconographic representations alongside explanatory text means that, for many people, on-line documentation is entering a whole new world. With the emergence of multi-media, we are likely to see still more major changes. However, it is still necessary to exercise a certain amount of caution, and when making your decisions, you must not overlook the areas in which technology is lagging behind.

4.3   Choosing your documentation medium

How then do you decide on what is most appropriate for your needs?

Let us first summarise the options available to you: traditional books, simple on-line text keyed to fields and screens, more complex on-line text taking advantage of hypertext capabilities, and the sophistication of multi-media, bringing in sound and moving images. Your application may only require documentation using one of these media, but it is more likely that a combination of several approaches will be more appropriate.

Although in most documentation decisions one normally starts with the user, in this case we must start with the system. You may be restricted by the limitations of the technology available to you.

If you are providing documentation for a mainframe or mid-range system and have users with traditional terminals rather than PC front-ends, hypertext and multi-media are not options available to you. In addition, your ability to illustrate any on-line text will be extremely limited. In this case, a combination of simple on-line help and a series of books is likely to be the most appropriate solution. The on-line text can be used to provide a brief overview for each screen and more detailed field help, and this can be supported by hard-copy documentation explaining how the different elements of the system are linked together, and how to use the options provided by the system to meet specific commercial objectives.

If your users have a sophisticated PC front-end, and it is still a luxury not afforded to many, your options are wider, although it is still unlikely that they will have access to PCs with the specification required to run multi-media applications. It is likely that this sort of support will be confined to training rooms and sales and marketing departments for a while yet.

At this stage, therefore, you must start to consider the needs of your users and any constraints imposed by their familiarity, or otherwise, with the technology. You may decide that the combination of simple on-line text and books as described above is still the most appropriate solution. It will depend entirely on your particular set of circumstances.

It is still difficult to overcome the problem of reflecting users' precise needs on-line without using sophisticated hypertext tools. To some extent, the champions of hypertext systems could argue, and quite rightly, that their methods *do* transcend options. I think, as a result, that hypertext will become more common in the future. But, and it is a big but, hypertext is complicated to develop and complicated to use. You need a very tidy mind at all stages, and the minds whose tidiness you cannot be sure of most are those of the users. They may not make the cognitive connections from where they 'are' to where they want to be as the developer of the text. They may also find the mechanics of hypertext systems more complex than their application software.

Set against this, hypertext offers powerful facilities, including the ability to maintain version control, to search by contents lists, word, phrase, or word proximity, and to follow hyperlinks - instant cross-reference jumps from one point in the text to another. The place where hypertext is likely to be most appropriate and accepted for a user guide will be in windows-type applications where the principles behind the workings of the help will be shared with those for other features of the system. Hypertext will also be of great value for holding very volatile, dynamic, and critically important information, such as standards and procedures. This means that any changes made are immediately available to all users, without any delay for the reissue for books.

There are a variety of different directions you can choose and the decision must be dictated by the circumstances in which you find yourself. You must, however, always remember that the documentation medium or selection of documentation media you choose must truly satisfy the needs of the audience, which can be both disparate and critical of technology.

5 The preparation of synopses and styleguides - the synergy of writing and design

In the earlier chapters we examined the true roles of the technical author - to write documentation that satisfies the practical needs of the reader, and papers over the cracks of actual or perceived imperfection in the computer system or service. We also saw how this principle dictated a radically new preparation method which concentrated on examining the computer system within the context of departmental requirements.

Obviously such an approach is vastly more likely to fail than a straight treatise on the supposed subject matter. An option by option account of a system can, by and large, only be structured and written in one way. A multiple volume departmental guide to a complex business function, on the other hand, sets itself up as a universal panacea, and if, as a result, there are eighteen titles - and there can be - there are, by implication, up to eighteen audiences to satisfy.

To reduce the risk of failure and retain the involvement of the end-user in the documentation process, a synopsis should be developed. This will establish the content and style of the book in some detail, stress the purpose of the document, and make clear to the reader which section of the company the book will be directed to.

When preparing a multi-volume set you may provide one synopsis for every book, where the style, content, and audience will vary considerably one to another. Alternatively, if you are writing a series of user guides that are similar in style, you may wish to describe them in a single synopsis so that common information is only described once. Of course, you may only be writing one book, and in this circumstance having to learn how to spell the plural of synopsis will not arise!

In some cases, systems are introduced into several sites, each of which has characteristics that are reflected in differing program building-blocks. In these situations, a policy decision will have to be made about whether all options should be included in a single guide, with a mechanism to indicate the requirements of each individual site to the user or, as an alternative, to develop a bespoke guide for every location. This is a subject about which much could be said, but here I will confine myself to stating that obviously it is critical that these decisions are made at the synopsis stage and that the documentation is structured accordingly.

In most instances, the synopsis should also include a 'styleguide'. This will show the prospective audience how the books will appear when they are 'published', including the types of illustration to be used.

You will see that I have drifted into calling the manuals guides, what you will - books. This is because there is a strong case for taking some of the exclusivity and preciousness out of computing activities - especially where non-computing user departments are concerned. Everyone knows what a book is!

It is important to stress that the person to whom the synopsis is presented - we will call him or her the reviewer - may not have seen any of the writer's work before and great care must be taken. The reviewer is usually pretty *au fait* with his or her work area, and confidence in the writer's skill will be dashed if there is ample evidence of carelessness in this crucial area.

5.1   An introduction to the synopsis

So what should a synopsis look like?

To some extent, this depends on the type of book that is being proposed. If the synopsis concerns a user guide, the section headings might not be as clearly defined as a standards and procedures manual. The former will explain broadly what will appear in every chapter and list each of the system options to be included, while the standards and procedures synopsis should define the section names by reference to individual standards and procedures.

Clearly, the reviewer of either type of synopsis must be able to check that everything has been covered -. a useful check for the writer.

5.2   The different aspects to consider

There are a number of crucial elements that must be included in any synopsis or series of synopses. Each of these is discussed in more detail below, but in summary they are as follows:

* style of writing, purpose, and audience
* a definition of the required book(s) and its (their) title(s)
* a description of the front matter
* a description of the main text and the method of pagination
* a description of the end matter.

The sections following include illustrations from a typical user guide synopsis for each of these areas.

5.3   The style of writing, purpose, and audience

The first thing to say here is that you may not have any choice in the matter of style. If you are working for a company that has already produced a range of documents, their writing style may be well established. Indeed, it may already be enshrined in a very detailed style guide, which lays out absolutely everything about the required style down to dotting the 'i's and crossing the 't's. If this is the case, unless you have a very good reason for not doing so, you must conform to the defined style and the synopsis should simply state that this is what you are doing.

If, however, you have some freedom in your choice of style, you should consider the points below.

The first decision to be made about the style of writing is whether the books are to be written in the second person or third person, and whether the text is to be active or passive voice.

To illustrate the point, let us take a single instruction written in a couple of different ways:

Second person, active voice

```
Enter a number in the range 25 to 50, and
then press Return.
```

Third person, passive voice

```
A number in the range 25 to 50 should be
entered. This must be followed by pressing
Return.
```

As you can see, second person, active voice gives the lightest feel to the statement. This writing style will sound like someone speaking over the user's shoulder giving advice and is by far the most friendly approach. Third person, passive voice, by contrast, is very distant and remote. This style is harder to read and is much less friendly.

Purpose of book and audience should be determined by your investigations; this is discussed in detail in an earlier chapter. These, together with the style of writing, must be clearly defined in the introduction to the synopsis (see Figure 5.1).

5.4   The front matter

Front matter will contain some, or all, of the following (see Figure 5.2):

• a copyright notice, complete with the © copyright mark

Figure 5.1
The synopsis
introduction

INTRODUCTION

This manual will be written in a friendly style using second person, active voice, i.e., as though the manual is addressing the reader directly.

The manual will be desktop published to the style shown in the styleguide section of this synopsis.

PURPOSE

The purpose of the manual is to:

- provide guidance to users entering orders into the system

- assist in the monitoring and control of orders

The overall intention is to provide users with a better understanding of the way in which they use the system, how their actions may impact on other users of the system, and to ensure that they are able to get the best out of the system.

AUDIENCE

The manual will be used by:

- Order entry clerks

- Order entry supervisors

It will be pitched at users with a basic understanding of the principles of their job, but with little or no experience of using a computer to assist in this task.

- a statement about copyright
- a liability notice
- a warranty notice
- acknowledgement of the use of trademarks in the document
- a by-line - always good for the writer's ego
- a thank-you to those who helped the writers in their task - always good for their egos!
- the name and address of the company whose product is being documented (the 'owner' of the book)
- the ISBN number, if the book is being published in the 'real' sense
- a version number of the document and, if appropriate, any associated software package's version number
- a welcome message or preface
- a contents sheet.

Most of these are self-explanatory. Where appropriate, the content of these is described in more detail later in this book, but it might be useful to dwell for a while on the reasons for the inclusion of one or two of these front matter items.

Copyright notice and statement

These are included to prevent unauthorised duplication of all or any part of the document without the owner's permission.

The liability and warranty notices

The liability and warranty notices protect the owner, and therefore, in these litigious times, the writer, from incorrect interpretation of the contents of the book. There have even been cases across the Pond where one division of a company has sued another division for supplying inaccurate documentation accompanying computer systems, so this clause can have a value well beyond the realms of the software house developing speculative products sold to third parties.

Trademarks

If your book contains names that are trademarks belonging to other organisations, you are legally obliged to acknowledge these at the beginning of the book.

Figure 5.2
The synopsis front matter description

FRONT MATTER

The book will include the following front matter:

Title page	This will show the name of the system, the name of the book, and any code name assigned to the book.
Copyright page/ Reproduction Restrictions	This page will include the standard copyright line, a statement that all rights are reserved, a statement detailing the reproduction restrictions, a liability notice and a warranty notice, and acknowledgment for the use of trademarks in the document. It will also acknowledge the assistance provided by PALL-OT personnel in the preparation of the book, and will name the author, primary editor, and designer of the book.
Contents page	This will list the chapters, the sections within each chapter, the index, and any appendices.

The welcome message or preface

The welcome message might appear in the first chapter or it may form a part of the front matter. The wording is often a bit of a selling exercise on the book and the system or service that it claims to explain.

5.5   The main text

The definition of the 'main text' in the context of this book is all the material between the front matter and the end matter - almost universally most of the book. What it will contain will depend on the title, the subject matter, and the audience.

5.5.1   Structure

An important aspect here is the structure of the document (see Figure 5.3). As in any book, chapters covering readily distinguishable topics are a good starting point. This proviso is all part of the objective to make finding things in the document straightforward. We have discussed at length the importance of seeing the system or service from the point of view of the reader. This being the case, the chapters should follow the mind of the reader, including the sequence and frequency of actions, rather than treating the book as an opportunity to bang on about the system.

As an example, an order processing system guide might have the following sequence of chapters.

Figure 5.3
Book structure

```
Chapter 1      Introduction

Chapter 2      Overview

Chapter 3      Entering orders for credit sales

Chapter 4      Entering orders for cash sales

Chapter 5      Changing order details

Chapter 6      Printing order details

Chapter 7      Maintaining customer records

Chapter 8      Making enquiries

Index
```

Those familiar with computer systems will immediately see the divergence here between purely systems requirements and the needs of the user. The aspects described in Chapters 3, 4, 5, and 6 are all likely to be part of a single computer program which facilitates the addition, amendment, deletion, and printing of orders. In contrast, Chapter 8 may describe enquiries on the customer, stock, order, and delivery files - drawing information from a number of different areas of the system.

Where the complexity of the system warrants it, the chapters can be further divided to avoid having more chapters than the Bible. I generally have a single level below the chapter which I call a section. I'm not keen on 'Parts' as I tend to think of these as superior to chapters and I tend to favour a different book altogether at this level. The books might be called parts, but I prefer a more appropriate title - Set-up, Reporting, Operation, Administrators' Guide, Credit Control Guide, etc. These titles mean much more to a reader than 'SoandSo System Documentation - Part 1'.

I certainly would not recommend documentation that resembles the structure of an international treaty - Volume 1, Part 16, Section 1, Subsection 6, Paragraph 146. This leads to absolutely horrendous pagination problems - the above paragraph appearing as 1,16,1,6,146 in any luckless contents page!

If you use a simple two-level structure, you can put all the chapters and sections in the contents sheet in a clear and well laid out way, that should go a long way to helping the reader. Remember, this is going to be a selfish read, where we must constantly respond to the question, 'I want', so we have to make rapid reader gratification a prime objective.

In a complex sales order processing system where there are dozens of aspects not mentioned in the contents list shown above, for example, one of these chapters might be structured as shown in Figure 5.4.

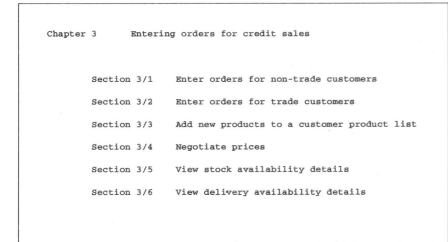

```
Chapter 3        Entering orders for credit sales


        Section 3/1    Enter orders for non-trade customers

        Section 3/2    Enter orders for trade customers

        Section 3/3    Add new products to a customer product list

        Section 3/4    Negotiate prices

        Section 3/5    View stock availability details

        Section 3/6    View delivery availability details
```

Figure 5.4
Chapter structure

5.5.2   *Pagination*

You have three choices for pagination: sequential, by chapter, or by section within chapter. When making your decision, you need to look carefully at the way in which the book is to be maintained and reissued. If the book is to be printed and issued in thousands of copies, and will be reissued in the same way with controlled releases of the software, you may wish to consider sequential pagination. If this is not the case, sequential pagination is not a good idea. For books that change frequently and/or are issued and reissued in relatively small numbers, pagination is best handled by numbering pages within chapters or, if sections are employed, numbering within sections within the chapter. Complicated? Not really. If sections and chapters are numbered within themselves, maintenance of the book is made infinitely more simple than having to reprint a book completely when a change or addition is made to the contents. This is, of course, assuming that a flexible form of book 'packaging' is adopted - such as using ring binders.

Where chapters do not warrant the inclusion of separate sections, pagination, can, obviously, be at chapter and page level only. For example, Chapter 4, page 10 might be written 4-10. Where a section is included, it is generally easier to number within section. For example Chapter 5, section 2, page 19, could be written 5/2-19. There is an infinite number of possibilities, but you should try to keep such systems consistent and easy for the reader to follow.

5.5.3   *The chapters*

Chapter 1 should almost always be an introduction. This should not be an introduction to the product or service. It is an introduction to the books. This is particularly important where several volumes have been prepared to reflect different tasks in the company, and stages in the life of the system. A diagram showing the way the books all complement each other should be included, as should an explanation of diagrams and symbols you are going to use in the main body of the text. A sample page should also be included.

There is sometimes doubt as to whether these opening words are ever read, but we have conclusive evidence that, if they are sufficiently diagrammatic, they will be read. Also, if there is no excuse for misunderstanding the structure and devices you have used, what might be termed 'silly queries' at the help desk, or equivalent, can be gently rebuked. It is so much easier to refer the puzzled user to the manual if the support team know that the manual is good and self-explanatory.

It is also a good idea to incorporate an overview chapter early on in the book. This is an overview of the system or service that you are documenting. This, of course, will be written within the context of the audience you are writing for. It will, therefore, be for the order taker in an order processing discipline, the credit controller in a credit checking routine. It will NOT be a long sermon describing the whole system for all and sundry. This, if it is required, would be contained in a separate document which would act as an introduction to the whole product or process. Remember, the purpose of user documentation is to inform, not educate - and there is a difference. Education is an academic process, ranging across the whole subject and telling the reader what *you* want them to know, whereas to inform is to tell the reader what he or she needs to know - quite a different objective.

All subsequent chapters, with their associated sections where these are justified, should cover a discrete topic. You should remember that the book is intended to be user and task driven, and you should title sections by the tasks to be performed and not the system option title (unless this matches the task, e.g. maintaining customer records). You may prefer not to name sections at this stage, but wait until the writing stage when you will have a fuller understanding. Whether or not you name the sections, it is essential that you provide a brief description of the contents of each chapter, a list of the system options to be described in the chapter, and mention any other points that you feel it is important to include in this area. Remember that the synopsis is intended to be a guide to both you and the reviewer so that you both have a clear understanding of what the content of the finished book will be (see Figure 5.5).

THE CHAPTERS

Chapter 3 - ENTERING ORDERS FOR CREDIT SALES

This chapter will provide sections describing the different options that may be used when processing credit sales. Several of the tasks described involve use of the same option, accessing the screens required by pressing a series of function keys. Where this is the case, the section will start with an illustration that shows the sequence of keys to be depressed to take you to the relevant screen.

This chapter will include sections with the following titles:

- Enter orders for non-trade customers
- Enter orders for trade customers
- Add new products to a customer product list
- Negotiate prices
- View stock availability details
- View delivery availability details

The options described in this chapter will be:

- Order entry
- Stock levels
- Planned delivery capacity

Figure 5.5
The synopsis chapter description

5.5.4   Using question and answer techniques

You may think that the chapter and section headings shown earlier to some extent contradict what I have been saying about making a book 'user friendly'. It seems all of a sudden to be about the topic in question rather than the user's requirements. One way around this is to structure the book in the form of questions - the trick being to make sure that the questions are exactly the sorts of queries posed by the reader. This approach is fine and you could translate most of the sections in Chapter 3 quite successfully. 'Enter orders for trade customers' would become, for example, 'How do I enter orders for trade customers?'

An obvious way to do this would be to use the questions as the section titles. This, however, can raise some problems with the readability of the contents sheet. If we take one of the examples shown above, you may see the problem (see Figure 5.6). As you can see, the titles become rather anonymous and harder to identify.

Other problems arise with the question and answer technique when dealing with the more obscure options.

For example, a section or chapter called 'User Access'. All right, you say, call it 'How do I access the system?' Fair enough, if this is what 'user access' means. But it probably doesn't. Those familiar with computer systems will know that user access is often about establishing authorities to access the system - the setting up of user profiles into which users are allocated, and the creation and alteration of passwords within the allotted access level - as well as the simple, 'How do I sign on?'

Now you could have a multiplicity of chapters and sections that break down every possible query under the general heading of 'user access'. 'How do I (a user) access the system?', 'How do I (a supervisor) award access to the system

Figure 5.6
The problems of using questions as titles

```
Chapter 3        How do I enter orders for credit sales?


        Section 3/1    How do I enter orders for non-trade
                       customers?

        Section 3/2    How do I enter orders for trade customers?

        Section 3/3    How do I add new products to a customer
                       product list?

        Section 3/4    How can I use the system when negotiating
                       prices?

        Section 3/5    How do I view stock availability details?

        Section 3/6    How do I view delivery availability
                       details?
```

to a user?', 'What is a user, in this context?', 'How do I provide access to an existing user at a different level of authority?', 'How do I alter my password?' (part of user access, surely?), 'How do I, a supervisor, alter the password/remove the password of another?' Neatly avoiding the obvious argument for two titles in this scenario - a user guide and a supervisor's manual - there could clearly be a plethora of entries in our contents sheet that would quite disconcert the user.

I favour question and answer books, but recognise it is a little difficult to reconcile questions with chapter headings, and speedy access from the contents list is very important. The way around this is to resort to an additional chapter at the beginning of the book - after the contents of course - which is devoted to the questions that arise, with a reference to the page on which the query is satisfied (see Figure 5.7). Try to group questions together in a logical order - preferably by type of task - and, if appropriate, use headings to identify the different groups.

In a question and answer book there are effectively two contents sheets - conventional and Q&A. Surely, when you have gone to this much trouble there can be no excuse for not finding what one is looking for!

Figure 5.7
The question-driven contents sheet

QUESTIONS

This chapter provides a list of questions that are answered in this book. This will help you to locate the information you require. For each question the number of the section in which the answer may be found is shown. The questions are grouped together in common subject areas.

ORDER PROCESSING

QUESTION	SECTION
How do I access a non-trade customer and enter a credit sale order?	3/1
How do I access a trade customer for order entry?	3/2
How do I access a customer and enter a cash sale order?	4/1
How do I add new products to a customer product list?	3/3
How can I use the system when negotiating prices?	3/4
How do I view stock availability details?	3/5
How do I view delivery availability details?	3/6

5.6   The titling of the books

The other thing I might mention at this stage is the titling of the books. It is all very well for *us* to talk in terms of 'books', but you have to put something on the cover - and it won't be 'book'. We haven't quite reached the point where a document describing an order processing system could be called 'The Book of the Gradgrind & Flywheel Order Processing System' - although, now I mention it, I cannot see why. There is a great tendency to add the word 'manual' or 'guide' to the title, viz., The Sales Ledger Manual, The General Ledger Reference Guide, etc.

On the whole these words are superfluous and they can be dangerous. They formalise things too much and, in so doing, push the reader away from the subject under discussion. To the average computer system user, a manual is something that tells you how to hang wallpaper, make an organic waste clamp, or bleed the brakes on a Reliant Robin - tasks that are boring or unsavoury - or both. If you must use a word, use 'guide', which at least has connections with pleasure activities and seems consequently lighter and warmer. Otherwise, just put 'Credit Control' or 'Sales Ledger', reserving the word 'guide' for the books associated with particular trades or professions - many of which will be associated with computer people who will not be so sensitive to titling - for example, 'The System Manager's Guide', 'The Administrator's Guide', 'The Supervisor's Guide'.

5.7   Preparing the styleguide

In terms of user guides, one cannot look at design in isolation from the writing. The page layout adopted will impact crucially on the writing style and the writer should have a great deal of input to the overall design. In our organisation we are lucky enough to have our own designer who creates all our book layouts. This section, therefore, is written in terms of a writer working closely with a designer.

If you are not in this fortunate position, you may have to play the part of both writer and designer. Design is, of course, a huge area, and it would be impossible to learn everything about it from a book. There are, however, some basic principles you should follow. In the next chapter we provide some pointers for this, and describe the different constraints and considerations for you when planning a layout for your book.

The styleguide is a very important part of the synopsis, as it is impossible to truly show, and gain agreement for, a writing style without reference to the general appearance of the books. In many companies the style, in terms of appearance, page size, structure, and binder, is the subject of a previously undertaken corporate design exercise and any drastic changes would be frowned upon. Even where the corporate image does not cater for computer system manuals, the degree of flexibility available to the author may be strictly limited. This does not, however, obviate the need for the presentation of a styleguide as part of the synopsis. Let me explain.

If a user guide is to be in a traditional style - A4 page size with very few diagrams to support the text - there will, perforce, have to be a great many words. Even if the document is written to satisfy commercial objectives and driven by a question and answer style, Figure 5.8 may be seen as a typical example of the likely structure.

```
NEGOTIATE PRICES

Price negotiation is one of the facilities provided by the order
entry option. You access this option on your computer system as
follows:

*   Select option 3, Order processing, from the main menu.

*   Select option 5, Order entry, from the Order processing menu.

When you are taking an order from a trade customer, you can
negotiate product prices to a limit set by the Sales Manager. If
you are prevented from entering the discount required by the
customer, refer them to your Supervisor.

When you negotiate a price you must:

1   Enter the details into the computer system and identify
    whether the customer accepts the price and places an order.

2   Print the price negotiation slip

3   Give the price negotiation slip to your Supervisor.

When you select the Order entry option, you access the price
negotiation screen as follows:

*   enter a customer code on the Customer Selection screen, and
    press Return,

*   enter the number of items required on the Order Entry screen,
    and press F18.

The following screen will be displayed:


                    price negotiation screen


You must complete the Accepted, User code, Password, and Unit
price fields before you will be allowed to exit from this screen.

The details you should particularly note on this screen are as
follows:
```

Figure 5.8
Section from a traditional word-processed manual

Figure 5.8 *(cont.)*

```
Credit Status
This field shows the credit status of the customer. This will be
Normal for normal status, Held if the order can be taken for the
customer but goods will not be released until authorised by
credit control, or Stop which indicates that you cannot take an
order for the customer.

Credit
This field shows the available credit for the customer.

Accepted
Enter Y in this field if the price you offer is accepted by the
customer. Otherwise, N.

User code
Enter your user code.

Password
Enter your user password.

Recommended price
This field shows the recommended retail price for the product.

Unit price
Enter the price you offer to the customer.

When you have completed your entries, press F10 to print the
price negotiation details. When the screen is redisplayed, press
Enter to leave the screen and return to the menu. If the price is
accepted, you will be prompted to confirm the order.

The details you enter here will impact on other areas of the
system. If the order is accepted, the order will be generated and
the items will appear on the picking report for the stores
department.
```

Fairly turgid stuff, you probably feel, and I would agree. To keep things simple, I have made assumptions about authority and access to the screen, confirmation of changes to a database record, and the method the user must adopt for moving the cursor around the screen. These might be covered in an introductory chapter or, unfortunately, they might expand the above text even more.

You might, however, have noticed the plus-point of the references to non-computing activities in the above example. These make all the difference to the acceptability of the book to an end-user.

Clearly, if such a text-heavy style is going to be adopted, the reviewer will need to know what he is letting himself in for, and including an example of the text in the context of the style in the synopsis will protect the writer from any future flak. In the above example, the text stands on its own without the design considerations and a reviewer of the synopsis could not be criticised for signing it off as broadly acceptable.

Even seen with a layout using desktop publishing to 'lift' pages, and including screen illustration as shown in Figure 5.9, the prospective end user will realise that some hefty reading will soon be coming his way.

Figure 5.9
A desktop-published
version of the
traditional text

NEGOTIATE PRICES

Price negotiation is one of the facilities provided by the order entry option. You access this option on your computer system as follows:

- Select option 3, Order processing, from the main menu.

- Select option 5, Order entry, from the Order processing menu.

When you are taking an order from a trade customer, you can negotiate product prices to a limit set by the Sales Manager. If you are prevented from entering the discount required by the customer, refer them to your Supervisor.

When you negotiate a price you must:

1. Enter the details into the computer system and identify whether the customer accepts the price and places an order.

2. Print the price negotiation slip.

3. Give the price negotiation slip to your Supervisor.

When you select the Order entry option, you access the price negotiation screen as follows:

- enter a customer code on the Customer Selection screen, and press Return,

- enter the number of items required on the Order Entry screen, and then press F18.

The following screen will be displayed:

```
PALL-OT Test System

OP986J           Order Entry Price Negotiation        ENTER      16/01/93

Customer G8736365  Order No. 072327  Credit Status Normal Credit    800.00
Accepted  Y          User code        Password              Agreed

Product    Quantity    Target    Unit       Total Line
                       Price     Price      Price
XL947467      10        50.00     48.00      480.00






F10 - Print negotiation slip
```

Figure 5.9 *(cont.)*

You must complete the Accepted, User code, Password, and Unit price fields before you will be allowed to exit from this screen.

The details you should particularly note on this screen are as follows:

Credit Status

This field shows the credit status of the customer. This will be Normal for normal status, Held if the order can be taken for the customer but goods will not be released until authorised by credit control, or Stop which indicates that you cannot take an order for the customer.

Credit

This field shows the available credit for the customer.

Accepted

Enter Y in this field if the price you offer is accepted by the customer. Otherwise, N.

User code

Enter your user code.

Password

Enter your user password.

Recommended price

This field shows the recommended retail price for the product.

Unit price

Enter the price you offer to the customer.

When you have completed your entries, press F10 to print the price negotiation details. When the screen is redisplayed, press Enter to leave the screen and return to the menu. If the price is accepted, you will be prompted to confirm the order.

The details you enter here will impact on other areas of the system. If the order is accepted, the order will be generated and the items will appear on the picking report for the stores department.

Let us now think of the same example where a highly illustrated style is going to be adopted in order to reduce the amount of text. Again, we will show first the text only - devoid of the symbols that will have to be used to support the text. Then we will show the same with the full styling.

Clearly, on its own, the example shown in Figure 5.10 makes little sense at all. There seems to be no 'bridge' between the instruction to do things on the computer and the display of the first screen. Following this, the list of field names in isolation is equally unhelpful. Finally, although the text refers to updating the picking list, it does not indicate which department this affects.

```
NEGOTIATE PRICES

MAIN MENU - 03  ORDER PROCESSING  - 05 ORDER ENTRY

When you are taking an order from a trade customer, you can
negotiate product prices to a limit set by the Sales Manager. If
you are prevented from entering the discount required by the
customer, refer them to your Supervisor.


When you negotiate a price you must:

Enter the details into the computer system and identify whether
the customer accepts the price and places an order.

Print the price negotiation slip

Give the price negotiation slip to your Supervisor.


Customer Selection

Enter Customer

Return

Order Entry

Enter number

F18

The following screen will be displayed:

price negotiation screen


Accepted

User code

Password

Unit price


CREDIT STATUS

This field shows the credit status of the customer. This will be
Normal for normal status, Held if the order can be taken for the
customer but goods will not be released until authorised by
credit control, or Stop which indicates that you cannot take an
order for the customer.
```

Figure 5.10
Text only for a section in a highly illustrated book

Figure 5.10 (*cont.*)

CREDIT

This field shows the available credit for the customer.

ACCEPTED

Enter Y in this field if the price you offer is accepted by the customer. Otherwise, N.

USER CODE

Enter your user code.

PASSWORD

Enter your user password.

RECOMMENDED PRICE

This field shows the recommended retail price for the product.

UNIT PRICE

Enter the price you offer to the customer.

To print the price negotiation details.

Enter to leave the screen and return to the menu. If the price is accepted, you will be prompted to confirm the order.

If the order is accepted, the order will be generated and the items will appear on the picking report.

The reviewer of the example above, were it included without a full styleguide, would be doing himself a disservice if he signed it off as being acceptable.

Now we will look at the above example in the context of its design characteristics (see Figure 5.11).

Naturally, elsewhere we will have explained that the exclamation mark indicates the critical fields on the screen that must be dealt with to satisfy the commercial objective in question, the computer symbol indicates computer tasks, the envelope denotes a clerical activity, and the S in a circle refers to the stores department.

The actual symbols used are of little significance providing they are agreed as part of the overall design considerations and, of course, they are easy to draw! It would be a good idea to adopt symbols that do mean something, however, as obscure images will counter the benefits to be gained from providing graphic 'clues'.

From this, it will be clear that an informed judgement about writing style, content, expansive explanation, etc., which the end-user must make during the synopsis stage, does depend on giving the potential reader the full story. It will also be clear that the text can be very considerably reduced where intelligent use of diagrams is included.

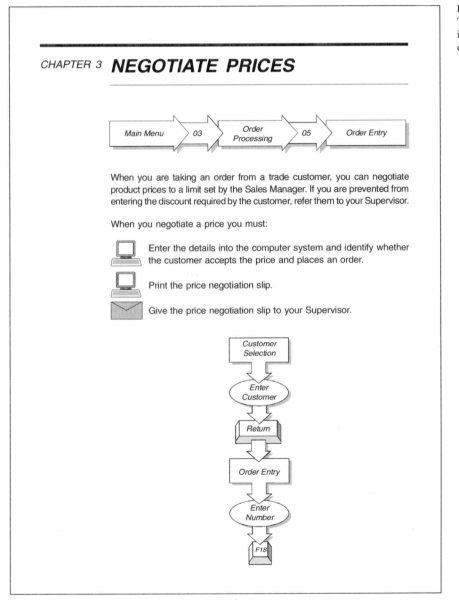

Figure 5.11
The illustrated version including all the diagrams

Figure 5.11 *(cont.)*

The following screen will be displayed:

```
PALL-OT Test System

OP986J            Order Entry Price Negotiation        ENTER    16/01/93

Customer G8736365  Order No.072327  Credit Status Normal Credit  800.00

Accepted  Y        User code        Password            Agreed


Product    Quantity    Target      Unit       Total Line
                       Price       Price      Price

XL947467    10         50.00       48.00       480.00







F10 - Print negotiation slip
```

> ! Accepted
>   User code
>   Password
>   Unit price

CREDIT STATUS	This field shows the credit status of the customer. This will be Normal for normal status, Held if the order can be taken for the customer but goods will not be released until authorised by credit control, or Stop which indicates that you cannot take an order for the customer.
CREDIT	This field shows the available credit for the customer.
ACCEPTED	Enter Y in this field if the price you offer is accepted by the customer. Otherwise, N.
USER CODE	Enter your user code.
PASSWORD	Enter your user password.
RECOMMENDED PRICE	This field shows the recommended retail price for the product.
UNIT PRICE	Enter the price you offer to the customer.

Figure 5.11 *(cont.)*

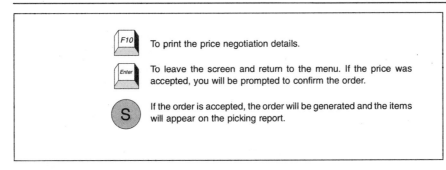

To print the price negotiation details.

To leave the screen and return to the menu. If the price was accepted, you will be prompted to confirm the order.

If the order is accepted, the order will be generated and the items will appear on the picking report.

One thing to be careful about when preparing the styleguide is the text to be used. Clearly text is needed, or else the relationship between illustration and text will be lost on the reviewer. However, there are dangers when you try to write a small section of the book ahead of acceptance of the style and synopsis. You may find that the reviewer concentrates on the content of your words rather than making a style and design judgement, together with reviewing the future content of the books as explained in the synopses. You then find yourself moving quickly onto the defensive, 'No, I know that is not ACTUALLY how you do that aspect. It is just here as a sort of example.'

Not good.

Some people try to get round this by writing text that acts as instructions on how the reviewer should be undertaking this task. For example, saying, 'text in this area will explain the operation of the option in the context of the user's commercial requirements'. The trouble with this approach is that the space is never of the right length for the explanation. Other people use what designers call 'Greek', although it always, to my classically untrained eye, looks more like Latin. This is, in fact, gobbledegook which forces the reviewer away from the content and onto the look and feel of the book.

Neither of these two solutions will really indicate to the reviewer how the text and design will work together. It really is worth investing a little time to find out *exactly* how one section (or part section) of the book will work and using this as an example.

5.8 Preparing visuals

Sometimes, and particularly where the design process is being undertaken in a greenfield site, there is a need for the preparation of a full set of visuals. This will involve the designer in much sticking and gluing, as the purpose behind the exercise is to prepare what is, effectively, a working model of the book.

Where all is new, the writer has an opportunity to experiment with a design approach that results in the need for minimalist text and I can only remember a single occasion when a managing director of a company said that he wanted long books because long books equalled comprehensive and full-featured products! As a result of the move towards less wordy tomes, design has become very important indeed.

All the design attributes will be present in the visual. The page size, examples of the font you wish to adopt, logos, headers and footers, use of screen images, and main and subordinate headings. You will also be advised to 'bulk' out the example. This means giving it a third dimension, as some people find it difficult to visualise how a book will 'feel' unless it can be shown proud of the backing sheet.

It may not be possible to show all the alternatives in font and layout you would like your owner to consider on the main visual example, so it is quite acceptable to supply extra pages showing the alternatives. These choices need to be explained very carefully indeed, or you may get an overall acceptance for a real mixture of styles!

6 Some basic lessons in document design

The design of a book must be an interactive process. It must take into consideration any constraints imposed by the owner, the reviewer, and the writer, as well as any personal preferences of the person implementing the design. For the sake of the descriptions in this chapter, we will call this person the designer. This need not necessarily be anyone professionally trained in this field, but it would help! You need to bear in mind, if recruiting someone for this purpose, that book design is a specialist skill in its own right within the design area.

Think of a user guide and the chances are you will imagine a blue binder full of pages - close-typed, no diagrams, and unread. Your 'thought' would be more or less accurate, since most user documentation reflects this rather unfortunate image.

Not that I have anything against blue binders as such, but so much more can be achieved when a desktop publishing system is used.

When designing a layout for a book, whether it is word-processed or desktop-published, the designer (or writer if you do not have a designer) must develop a styleguide. This was mentioned in the context of the synopsis in the last chapter, but I will enlarge upon the subject here. In addition to the details described in the previous chapter, the styleguide sets out such things as page size, heading weights, gutters and margins, typefaces, and a range of other details.

These may sound like difficult concepts and giving an understanding of all aspects of book design is far more than a single chapter in a book like this could hope to achieve. But, for those who are not designers and yet have been set the task of implementing a book design, I hope it will give you some useful pointers.

6.1 Corporate standards

Just as the writer must adhere to any standards established by the owner for the style of the book, so must the designer. The first thing that the designer must look at is whether the owner has any corporate standards for design and style of documents. Particularly in large companies, these can be very strict and *must* be adhered to. If they specify that Helvetica 10 point must be used for all standard text and Helvetica 20 point must be used for headings, the designer has no choice - this is the way it must be.

Some companies will have produced quite a large glossy book to describe their corporate design standards. If this is the case, it is essential that the designer obtains a copy of this to determine what is required - it will usually be held in the marketing department or the publications department. It will lay out all the defined standards in some detail, including the size, weight, and quality of paper to be used for final production. It could even go so far as to say that a special alphabet set specific to the company in question must be used, in which case you will have to ensure that your chosen tools can use this. If the owner has a logo that must be used, there will be restrictions and specifications about the size, colours used, how it must appear when shown in black and white, and where it may appear on a page. All of this information will appear in the corporate design guide.

The designer and writer must also remember to ascertain whether there are any corporate standards for the tools used to carry out the job. If the owner has standards for word processing, desktop publishing, and drawing packages, again, they must be followed.

If the books are being produced for a company with an existing documentation department, it is quite possible that it has a very precise style rule book that specifies everything in minute detail. This will include not only the overall corporate constraints, but also those for their user documentation, including specific typographical devices, such as bullet points. In this case the designer may as well pack up his bags - the design task has been done already - and all that is required is to produce the book to the existing standards.

Some companies may have corporate standards for letter heading, brochures, etc., but nothing specifically for documentation of the sort we are considering. In this case the designer must tread carefully. It is a good idea to use the existing corporate standards wherever possible, but it is also well worth spending time determining who has overall responsibility for this aspect of things in the company, and ensuring that they give approval for the finished design - otherwise the reviewer may make decisions that are later vetoed.

6.2   Considering the users' environment

Once any corporate standards requirements have been established, and providing the designer is allowed a certain amount of freedom, the next area to look at is the environment in which the document will be used. This will govern a number of elements such as the final size of the book as well as the layout. For example, books that are to be used in a computer department may well be best produced in A4 format - the same as all the others held there. The people in this area are used to this format and something smaller might well get lost. On the other hand, a book to be produced for a busy nursing station in a hospital environment should be small so that it does not clutter up the desk, and the appearance inside the book must be very light and encouraging. After all, nurses want to look after their patients rather than use computer systems and there will be quite enough on the desk at the nursing station without adding a huge text-heavy book that looks so discouraging that it is never used.

The designer also needs to have an eye out for considerations for the final production method and materials at this stage - but more of that in a later chapter.

6.3   Working with the writer

Having looked at the owner's and the users' requirements, the designer must then turn to the writers and see what needs they have. Some of these considerations were discussed in the styleguide section of the synopsis chapter, but it is worth mentioning them again here.

The considerations will include:

- the elements into which the book is divided - chapters or sections
- the number of heading levels used
- whether heading levels are numbered
- whether attention needs to be drawn to special notes in the text
- the typefaces to be used - both for main text and for screens, reports, and other illustrations
- how symbols are to be used
- how diagrams are to be used
- whether any text needs lifting for emphasis, e.g. using bold or italic characters to emphasise field or key names
- the need for running headers and footers
- use of tables and columns
- basic text layout.

6.4   Creating the design

The designer should by this stage have all the basic information at his fingertips and now be ready to start the design.

Just as an artist starts with a blank canvas, so the book designer begins with a single white page. Like the artist, the designer must paint a picture on that page that will be appealing to the eye. Their 'paints', however, will be quite different. Whereas the artist will be working in oils, watercolours, pastels, acrylics, and the like, and creating in all the colours of the rainbow, the book designer will be working with text and graphics and, most likely, a very restricted set of colours (often just black and white).

6.4.1   *Page size*

The designer must first choose the size of the page, taking into consideration any standards already in existence, the environment in which the book will be used, and the cost constraints. Obviously if the owner has existing bound documentation and wishes to use standard binders, these will govern the size selected. If this is not the case, other considerations come into play.

The page size for a book can be defined specifically for a document set. It is not necessary to conform to one of the standard international paper sizes. If the designer wishes to use a size between A4 and A5, as found in many PC manuals, this is entirely possible. There will, however, be a cost implication in this - and a green issue. If a paper size outside the international standards is chosen, the pages will have to be trimmed down from one of the standard sizes. The resultant waste means that the paper is used much less economically.

6.4.2   *Balance and proportion*

The successful landscape artist, sitting on his stool gazing out over rolling countryside on a bright spring day, must, at an early stage in the process, consider the balance and proportion of his picture. Not too much sky, but enough to set off the verdant landscape below. A hint of sunlight in the sky, but no great orb dominating the whole view.

In the same way, the balance and proportion of text and illustration on a page is very important to the whole 'feel' of a book. Good design in this area is rarely commented on, but we all spot a bad design immediately - it simply does not feel comfortable.

In good design, the text must not be allowed to fill the page completely. There must always be a border of 'white space' surrounding the text and illustration (see Figure 6.1). This space can be used to dramatic effect, particularly in large text-heavy tomes, where it can be used to give the page a lighter appearance that is easier on the eye.

Figure 6.1
Text and non-text areas

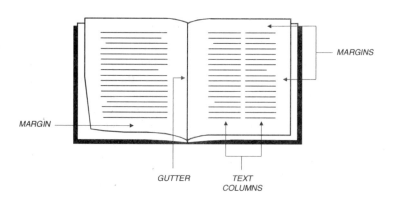

When planning the white space, there are rules to follow. Primarily, the text and illustration must look comfortable and balanced in the page. One element when working towards this is ensuring that there is more space below the text at the base of the page than there is above the text at the top of the page. The side margins should be balanced. If there is any imbalance, it should be because the gutter (the inner margin) is greater than the outer margin. This will be necessary in some situations, particularly where the book is to be drilled for loose-leaf binding.

6.4.3 Columns/grids

The grid is the area on the page where the basic text and illustration will be presented. The designer needs to decide how many columns are to be used in the grid and whether they are to be even or uneven (see Figure 6.1). You should remember that the columns are not columns as you or I usually think of them (as used in newspapers or tables), but text areas. Within these text areas you may have additional columnar text. To understand this you should look at the following two examples (Figures 6.2 and 6.3).

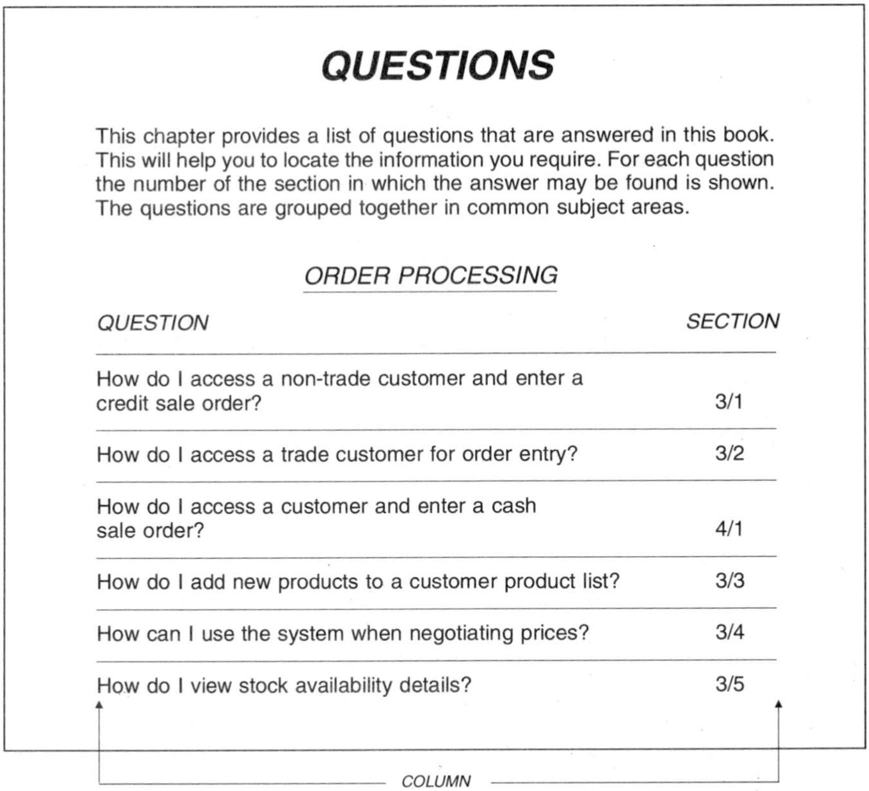

Figure 6.2
Single-column grid

QUESTIONS

This chapter provides a list of questions that are answered in this book. This will help you to locate the information you require. For each question the number of the section in which the answer may be found is shown. The questions are grouped together in common subject areas.

ORDER PROCESSING

QUESTION	SECTION
How do I access a non-trade customer and enter a credit sale order?	3/1
How do I access a trade customer for order entry?	3/2
How do I access a customer and enter a cash sale order?	4/1
How do I add new products to a customer product list?	3/3
How can I use the system when negotiating prices?	3/4
How do I view stock availability details?	3/5

COLUMN

Figure 6.3
Two-column grid

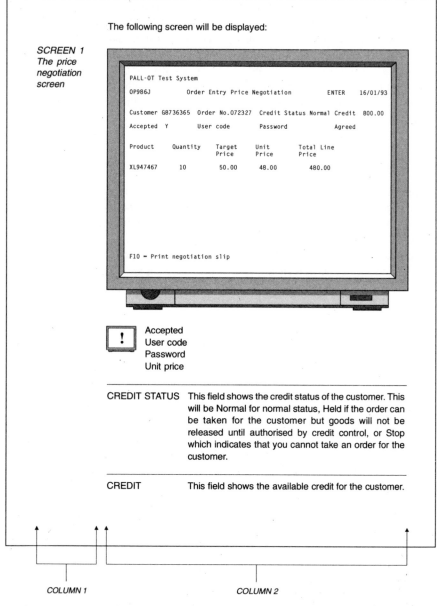

The following screen will be displayed:

SCREEN 1
The price
negotiation
screen

```
PALL-OT Test System

OP986J          Order Entry Price Negotiation          ENTER     16/01/93

Customer G8736365  Order No.072327  Credit Status Normal Credit  800.00

Accepted  Y        User code        Password           Agreed

Product      Quantity    Target     Unit      Total Line
                         Price      Price     Price
XL947467       10        50.00      48.00       480.00




F10 - Print negotiation slip
```

! Accepted
   User code
   Password
   Unit price

CREDIT STATUS   This field shows the credit status of the customer. This
                will be Normal for normal status, Held if the order can
                be taken for the customer but goods will not be
                released until authorised by credit control, or Stop
                which indicates that you cannot take an order for the
                customer.

CREDIT   This field shows the available credit for the customer.

COLUMN 1   *COLUMN 2*

As you can see, in the two-column style the first column is only used for items such as screen captions. The bulk of the text and illustration, even the clearly defined columns for the field descriptions, is held in the second column. This is a device that can be used in some situations to introduce extra white space and lighten the appearance of the page. In the general course of events, one- or two-column grids are the most appropriate for user documentation.

Further columns are usually only used for documents such as newsletters and newspapers.

When defining the column sizes, the designer must take a number of factors into consideration, including the type size used, the interline spacing, and the width of each line to be read. The last is extremely important. If a line of text is too wide, the readers' interest tails off as they scan across the page and it can be quite difficult for them to absorb the text at the end of the line and to follow the text to the start of the next line.

6.4.4   Typefaces

In the vast majority of books the greatest part of the book is type. As with the other elements of the design, the designer may be constrained by corporate standards. Even if standards exist where the owner has not produced this type of documentation before, the designer may find that these do not include a typeface suitable for book production. In this event an alternative must be agreed.

When selecting a typeface for a book, it is essential to select one that provides easy readability in a block of text. If you flick through a catalogue of typefaces you will see a wide range of decorative typefaces and some that are more appropriate, particularly with regard to size and line spacing, for use in documents. Many of the decorative typefaces are designed with a specific use in mind, others are just too flowery - more suitable for use on the top of a box of chocolates than in a user guide!

The designer will be well advised to stick to one of the well tried and tested standards for documentation. Good choices would be Helvetica for a sans serif selection, or Times for a serif selection (a serif typeface is one that utilises a small line at the main extremities of a main stroke in each type character). Times is a good example of a typeface appropriate to documentation since it was specifically designed for use in newspapers. For some indication of what these typefaces are like, Times New Roman (the New Roman indicates a variant on the original style) is the typeface used for the bulk of this book and Helvetica italic is used for the annotation of diagrams.

It is very important not to mix too wide a variety of typefaces on a page, particularly serif and sans serif typefaces. For example, it is quite acceptable to use Times for the main text and Helvetica in diagrams as has been done in this book, but it would look very messy if in addition the headings were set in Bodoni. Using too many typefaces simply looks unattractive.

Typefaces are generally available in a number of different sizes, termed 'point' sizes. Different sizes of type can be used to emphasise features such as headings, and to give lower priority to text providing annotation or header and footer detail.

Figure 6.4
Typeface weights and
attributes

Helvetica Medium	Times Medium
Helvetica Italic	*Times Italic*
Helvetica Bold	**Times Bold**
Helvetica Bold Italic	***Times Bold Italic***

As I indicated previously, there are variants on the typefaces (see Figure 6.4). The designer should pick one that includes a variety of weights and forms, e.g. bold, medium, light, and italic. This will provide a degree of flexibility for the use of the typeface - particularly important when trying to accommodate the requirements for items such as headings.

6.4.5   Headers and footers

The footer is usually a more important consideration than the header for a page. This is because the footer usually accommodates the page number. Page numbers may be shown in the header, as in this book, but this is rather an unnatural position for them in user documentation. Most of us read a user guide as a book rather than a newspaper and accordingly will expect to find page numbers at the foot of the page. In this section I have mainly addressed the question of footers, but similar considerations apply to headers.

One should remember here that a header is not the same as a heading. A heading is an important item on a page, whereas the header is only providing supplementary information. When using headers, the designer will have to take a decision about whether headers will conflict with headings that appear at the top of the page, and whether in these circumstances the header should be switched off (see Figure 6.5). If you flick through this book you will see that headers have been 'switched off' for the first page of each chapter.

The key detail with the footer is its position on the page. Together with the main body of the text, the footer makes a shape on the page. There are three possible positions for a footer relative to the main body of the text: aligned at the left-hand side, centred, or aligned at the right-hand side.

Figure 6.5
Header and footer
positions

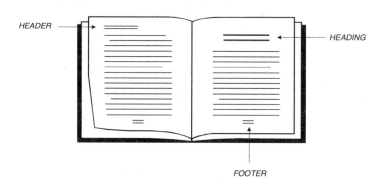

```
┌──────────────────────────────────────────────────┐
│                                                    │
│   PRENTICE HALL        3 - 1      OFFICE MANAGEMENT │
│   Copyright 1993                  Computer Operations │
│                                                    │
└──────────────────────────────────────────────────┘
```

Figure 6.6
The three-position footer

If necessary, because of the need to include several different types of information in the footer, there could be footer elements in all three positions (see Figure 6.6).

The other factor when considering footers is ensuring that they are clear and readable. Once a user has identified their requirements from a contents list or index, the footer is their guide into the book. For this reason, the page number element is usually positioned at the outer margin. It is also important that the footer does not contain too much information unless it is really necessary. The example provided above contains far more information than it is advisable to include in a footer, but is based upon one we had to devise to meet very specific client requirements.

You will have observed that headers and footers cut into the white space round the edge of the page. This is something to take into consideration when determining the page margins. When deciding on the positions for the headers and footers, the designer must again remember that the page must balance and the header or footer should be closer to the text than to the edge of the page. For non-standard page sizes this last point is very important as the pages will have to be trimmed to size by the printer. If the headers and footers are too close to the edge, you may sense a ghostly shadow of knitting needles clicking away outside the Bastille as the guillotine merrily chops off your headers!

6.4.6   Symbols and graphics

Any design to be presented for review must contain examples of the type of illustration to be incorporated. This will include both the diagram styling, and the use of icons and other graphics, e.g. screen surrounds.

This is a subject discussed in much more detail in the next chapter. The main point to note here is that, like everything else about the book, it is important to keep all illustration meaningful and simple. In terms of the overall design of the page, the design presented for review must show the positioning of illustrations on the page and their relationship to the text.

6.4.7   Other devices

A variety of devices can be used to improve the appearance of a page. For example, lines above and below a main heading can give it greater emphasis.

Figure 6.7
'Lifting' a sub-heading

BEFORE

Careful use of the 'attributes' such as point size, underlining, italicising, emboldening, and others, can greatly enhance the appearance of the text. They can be used to increase the readability and indicate the 'seniority' of the text.

Summary
If you, like me, are not an expert in this area, you may be throwing up your hands in horror by now.

AFTER

Careful use of the 'attributes' such as point size, underlining, italicising, emboldening, and others, can greatly enhance the appearance of the text. They can be used to increase the readability and indicate the 'seniority' of the text.

Summary

If you, like me, are not an expert in this area, you may be throwing up your hands in horror by now.

If a sub-heading appears positioned between two pieces of text, it needs to be 'lifted' from the text in some way. One way of doing this is to increase the point size of the sub-heading text and add a line beneath it (see Figure 6.7).

Careful use of the 'attributes' such as point size, underlining, italicising, emboldening, and others, can greatly enhance the appearance of the text. They can be used to increase the readability and indicate the 'seniority' of the text.

6.5   Summary

If like me you are not an expert in this area you may be throwing up your hands in horror by now. There are so many different things to take into consideration - corporate standards, users' environment, page size, white space, columns and grids, captions, typefaces, point sizes, annotation, weights and forms, headers, headings, footers, graphics, icons, and attributes. And this is all just a summary view!

I would simply be tempted to go and curl up in a dark corner somewhere and try to forget about it. But never fear, all is not doom and gloom. Help is at hand. Many of the desktop publishing packages on the market today come with some ready made templates which may be used either as they are or with minor modifications. This can be quite a good solution if you do not have the time or the skills to create designs of your own. There are simple answers to the problems of creating diagrams and other illustrations as well, as you will see in the next chapter.

So don't move on with a heavy heart. This is a specialist area, but you are not alone.

7 Obtaining diagrams and assembling a book

Writing the text is not the only task involved when preparing a book. If your book is to be a highly illustrated one, you may well be assembling examples of screens, reports, a number of diagrams, and other illustrative material during the writing exercise. All of these require careful consideration and the method by which you are going to obtain them must be established early in the project. If you are fortunate you may be working with a graphic designer or illustrator, and he or she may make a very valuable contribution to the process with all sorts of suggestions that may enable you to reduce the amount of text and generally make the book more appealing. The task of compiling the finished book can only be undertaken once all the text and illustrative material has been collated.

7.1 Screens and reports

Obtaining screen and report examples that are both sensible and in a form that you can use in your word-processed or desktop-published document can be complicated and politically sensitive. There are two aspects to this: ensuring that the data shown is meaningful, and determining the physical mechanism used to obtain appropriate files.

7.1.1 Obtaining good examples

Very often the screen and report examples available to the writers at the time they are supposed to be preparing the first drafts are rudimentary, to say the least. All the headings may be in place, but if working from program specifications, the detail lines will probably be filled with uninformative characters (see Figure 7.1) and if looking at test systems they might find lonely entries saying 'test' or 'fred bloggs', or worse. This is, of course, of no value whatsoever to the reader. A screen or report with symbols or characters indicating field lengths looks unattractive and will be very offputting to the user, who will *never* see it in that format. Similarly, a screen showing blank field entries will not really give the reader any clues, and may actually be misleading if the screen initially appears showing some defaults.

Figure 7.1
The program
specification screen
example

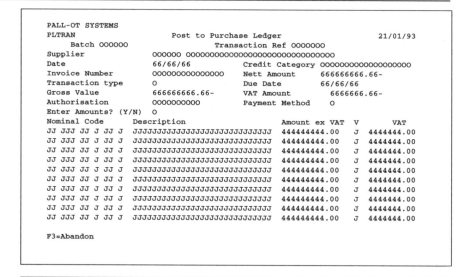

```
PALL-OT SYSTEMS
PLTRAN                        Post to Purchase Ledger              21/01/93
        Batch 000000                   Transaction Ref 0000000
Supplier              000000 00000000000000000000000000000000
Date                  66/66/66          Credit Category 000000000000000000000
Invoice Number        000000000000000   Nett Amount        666666666.66-
Transaction type      O                 Due Date           66/66/66
Gross Value           666666666.66-     VAT Amount           6666666.66-
Authorisation         0000000000        Payment Method     O
Enter Amounts? (Y/N)  O
Nominal Code          Description                 Amount ex VAT  V     VAT
JJ JJJ JJ J JJ J      JJJJJJJJJJJJJJJJJJJJJJJJJJJJJJJ  444444444.00   J  4444444.00
JJ JJJ JJ J JJ J      JJJJJJJJJJJJJJJJJJJJJJJJJJJJJJJ  444444444.00   J  4444444.00
JJ JJJ JJ J JJ J      JJJJJJJJJJJJJJJJJJJJJJJJJJJJJJJ  444444444.00   J  4444444.00
JJ JJJ JJ J JJ J      JJJJJJJJJJJJJJJJJJJJJJJJJJJJJJJ  444444444.00   J  4444444.00
JJ JJJ JJ J JJ J      JJJJJJJJJJJJJJJJJJJJJJJJJJJJJJJ  444444444.00   J  4444444.00
JJ JJJ JJ J JJ J      JJJJJJJJJJJJJJJJJJJJJJJJJJJJJJJ  444444444.00   J  4444444.00
JJ JJJ JJ J JJ J      JJJJJJJJJJJJJJJJJJJJJJJJJJJJJJJ  444444444.00   J  4444444.00
JJ JJJ JJ J JJ J      JJJJJJJJJJJJJJJJJJJJJJJJJJJJJJJ  444444444.00   J  4444444.00
JJ JJJ JJ J JJ J      JJJJJJJJJJJJJJJJJJJJJJJJJJJJJJJ  444444444.00   J  4444444.00
JJ JJJ JJ J JJ J      JJJJJJJJJJJJJJJJJJJJJJJJJJJJJJJ  444444444.00   J  4444444.00

F3=Abandon
```

Figure 7.2
A sensible screen
example

```
PALL-OT SYSTEMS
PLTRAN                        Post to Purchase Ledger              21/01/93
        Batch    1789                  Transaction Ref    456824
Supplier              ARC083 Arconium Mouldings Limited
Date                  18/01/93          Credit Category Standard Terms
Invoice Number        AS/89236          Nett Amount          1096.51
Transaction type      I                 Due Date           28/02/93
Gross Value              1288.40        VAT Amount            191.89
Authorisation         HAFNAP            Payment Method     C
Enter Amounts? (Y/N)  Y
Nominal Code          Description                 Amount ex VAT  V     VAT
10 503 45 1 95 6      Aluminium moulded goods          1000.00   S    175.00
10 503 45 1 95 7      Aluminium castings                 96.51   S     16.89




F3=Abandon
```

The standard response to pleas for a 'sensible' screen or report layout (see Figure 7.2) seems to be 'make it up yourself'. Now this is a very flawed response and shows a total lack of appreciation of what the writer is supposed to do. Writers write and they cannot be expected to work out the nuances of a complex report from a sample with abbreviated column headings and the word 'test' in the field below. If detective work to this level of detail is required, the schedules for document production will go out and therefore the cost of document preparation will rise very considerably.

It must be up to the system developers to provide sensible completed screen and report samples, but up to the writer to decide what is required to tell the reader the full story.

A word of warning should be added at this point. It may be tempting for the developers to obtain data from a 'tame' customer for use as illustration. Whilst this will undoubtedly give truly representative information, the writer must make sure that the customer has given their approval as the information may be commercially sensitive. One horror story I know of in this area concerned a company who produced a book describing all the reports available from their system, using a customer's information as the basis for their report examples. The project went all the way through to producing high quality, two-colour, printed copies before anyone thought to show it to the customer concerned. Although the writing team had changed seemingly critical details such as names, the customer was in such a specialist market that they felt that they could still be identified from the reports shown. Furthermore, the examples used would provide their competitors with valuable market intelligence. Every book had to be withdrawn and shredded, new examples found, and the book reprinted - a very expensive exercise!

7.1.2 Obtaining data in an appropriate file format

Having gained access to some reasonable data, it will then be necessary for the writer to find a means of obtaining this in a file format compatible with the writing and desktop publishing tools being used for the project.

There are two possibilities here. The first is that the tools used for system development provide facilities for obtaining the layouts required. You may find, however, that these tools will only provide the basic screen design and field descriptions - no data will be included.

Your second port of call must be screen and report 'grabbing' software. A number of proprietary packages are available that allow you to display an image on the screen and capture part or all of the image as a data file. These products usually allow you to select from a number of output formats. I would advise selecting a format that allows you to make amendments easily. This will ensure that the writer can make changes when he spots silly pieces of information, such as dates reading 99:99:99, or if the reviewers require minor changes.

7.1.3 Presentation

Assuming that you do not wish to follow the old-style word-processing methods of surrounding examples by asterisks or the like, you essentially have two options. The first is to surround the screen with a simple 'keyline' and the second is to surround it with a graphic image that reflects the actual screen or report (see Figures 7.3 and 7.4).

Figure 7.3
Screen with a keyline surround

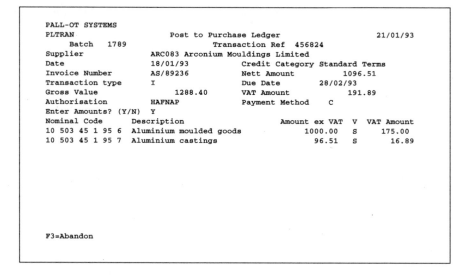

```
PALL-OT SYSTEMS
PLTRAN                          Post to Purchase Ledger                    21/01/93
        Batch    1789                      Transaction Ref  456824
Supplier                  ARC083 Arconium Mouldings Limited
Date                      18/01/93           Credit Category Standard Terms
Invoice Number            AS/89236           Nett Amount           1096.51
Transaction type          I                  Due Date        28/02/93
Gross Value                   1288.40        VAT Amount             191.89
Authorisation             HAFNAP             Payment Method     C
Enter Amounts? (Y/N)  Y
Nominal Code        Description                       Amount ex VAT  V  VAT Amount
10 503 45 1 95 6  Aluminium moulded goods               1000.00     S     175.00
10 503 45 1 95 7  Aluminium castings                      96.51     S      16.89




F3=Abandon
```

Figure 7.4
Screen with a graphic surround

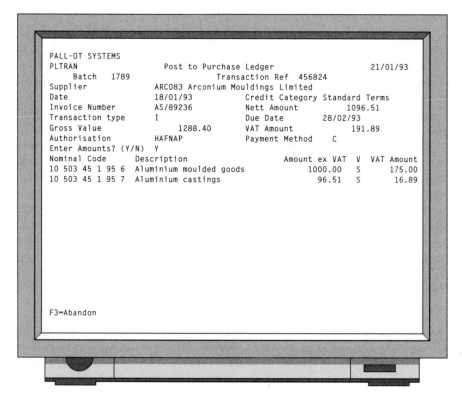

```
PALL-OT SYSTEMS
PLTRAN                          Post to Purchase Ledger                    21/01/93
        Batch    1789                      Transaction Ref  456824
Supplier                  ARC083 Arconium Mouldings Limited
Date                      18/01/93           Credit Category Standard Terms
Invoice Number            AS/89236           Nett Amount           1096.51
Transaction type          I                  Due Date        28/02/93
Gross Value                   1288.40        VAT Amount             191.89
Authorisation             HAFNAP             Payment Method     C
Enter Amounts? (Y/N)  Y
Nominal Code        Description                       Amount ex VAT  V  VAT Amount
10 503 45 1 95 6  Aluminium moulded goods               1000.00     S     175.00
10 503 45 1 95 7  Aluminium castings                      96.51     S      16.89




F3=Abandon
```

Using a graphic around the screen or report will lift the surrounding text and make the page more interesting to look at. However, set against this, there may be editorial constraints. Graphics generally have a fixed position in a file and will have to be moved if the length of the surrounding text changes. Although some desktop publishing tools (and pseudo-desktop publishing packages) allow you to anchor graphics to text, in general this does not work terribly well. On the other hand, keylines can usually be made part of the text file or the 'tagging' or mark-up language dictating its layout. They will, therefore, always move with the text. If you are dealing with long files that will require extensive editing, you may find it easier to use keylines than graphics.

7.2   Other illustrations

Illustrations may come in a number of forms: diagrams produced using a proprietary drawing package, images created by passing an existing illustration through a scanning device, photographs, and images drawn from a clip-art library. These can be enlarged or shrunk to suit the requirements of the document.

The first thing to say is that you should adopt illustrative techniques appropriate to your capabilities. Although a good drawing package can help, if you are not experienced in its use it is better to keep things simple. Many drawing packages now have templates available for the production of flow chart-type illustrations. These, together with images from clip-art libraries, should fulfil many of your requirements. If you are not experienced and require a diagram that is beyond your ability to create, you may be well advised to put the task out to a bureau that specialises in this type of service.

Although diagrams make a book more interesting to read, it is important that they are used to support and supplement the text and not just added at random. 'Gosh, we've had four pages without a diagram; I'd better put something in here,' is not a good approach to take. Superfluous illustration will simply irritate your reader.

There are a few golden rules when creating diagrams. Number one has to be keep it simple. Even if you are an expert with a drawing package, creating a diagram that looks like a complex spider's web with lines of flow going in all directions and annotation flying out at all angles will only confuse your reader. This is not to say that you cannot represent complex ideas in a diagram, but you should restrict the illustration to showing simple flows. If necessary, you may need to split the diagram into different component parts in order to simplify matters. If you look at the diagrams used in the early part of this book, you will see examples of this.

Figure 7.5
Bad annotation!

Figure 7.6
Good annotation

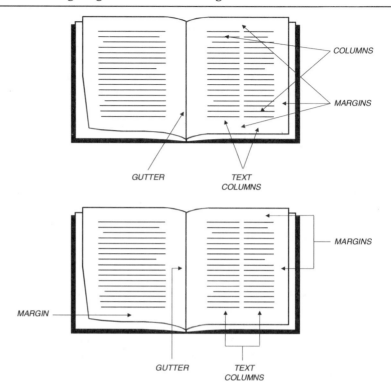

7.3 Annotation

Just as the diagram should be kept simple, so should any annotation. If there is too much annotation, you should be splitting the diagram into smaller component parts. Use all four sides of the diagram for annotation and, wherever possible, spread it evenly round the picture. This will ensure that it looks balanced on the page. A diagram with all the annotation on one side can look as precarious as the leaning tower of Pisa!

The leader lines taken in from the text to the point in the diagram to which the annotation refers should always be parallel to one of the sides of the page. If necessary, you may have a line with a right-angle in it in order to achieve this. Whatever you do, do *not* cross leader lines. This quickly becomes messy and difficult to follow (see Figures 7.5 and 7.6).

7.4 Assembling the book

So the design is established, the text has been prepared, and all the illustrative material required has been gathered together. It is now the task of the desktop publishing operator to lay out the book, fitting text and illustrations into the page format with care and sensitivity (see Figure 7.7).

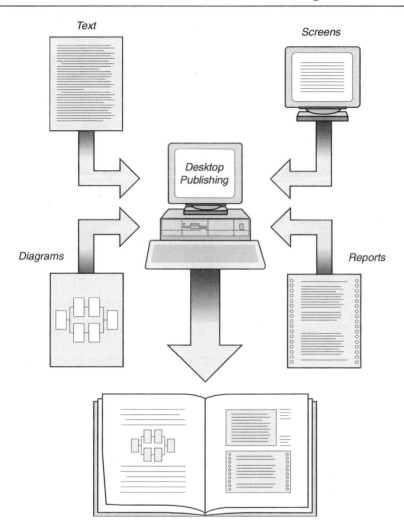

Figure 7.7
Assembling the book

For the sake of argument, I am assuming that the book is to be desktop-published. Even if it is not, the principles outlined in this section still apply.

The finished book should not have single lines on otherwise blank pages, nor should a screen be squashed into the page so that the footer is dominated by the screen frame. This may mean tweaking the text from time to time and it is legitimate for the desktop publisher to have the authority to do this. He must, however, if he is doing this, also look at the words to make sure that the effect of his work does not make a nonsense of the text; 'the screen below' when it is not below and so on. There may be occasions when the desktop publisher needs the second opinion of the writer concerning a design problem or the 'run' of the book and here it is useful for the writer to understand the problem in full. If nothing else, it will make the writer appreciate the complex task the desktop publisher is faced with.

In time, the last page will be slotted into place and the draft will be finished. Before the desktop publisher hands the book back to the writer he will give it a visual check after printing it out. As a result of this, there may be certain changes he wishes to make - either as a result of error or perhaps because, in the real world, he feels that an aspect of the layout or style and design does not really work exactly as he had hoped. If the change is significant, this may mean resorting to talking to the reviewer again, but the change is often very minor in the eyes of the uninitiated and there is no good reason to trouble the powers that be.

Oh, one final point. Under no circumstances should you overcome a text discrepancy with the number of pages in a book with the phrase, 'this page has been intentionally left blank'. The reader will never think otherwise!

8 The drafting process - three stages to a satisfactory conclusion

So far we have discussed the need for an investigative process that takes the practical requirements of the user into consideration, and the need to prepare a synopsis and style guide to indicate to the reviewer what he or she should expect to see. Obviously, the next stage is the actual writing of the book. At this point it seems appropriate to stand back a little and look at other stages in the process as these will have an impact on the way you approach the writing (see Figure 8.1).

Clearly, your work will need some pretty thorough editing before you release it formally to a reviewer, and this process is the subject of Chapter 10. However, you still need to ensure that, at the end of the day, the reviewer is happy with the final product. Unless you are both remarkably talented and unbelievably lucky, the document you first submit will contain errors and omissions which need to be corrected before text development can be considered to be complete.

In general, it is a good idea to adopt a multi-stage drafting process, where you submit a draft of the book for review and incorporate the reviewer's comments at each stage. I believe that keeping to three draft stages is the most efficient method and that is what will be discussed in this chapter. There will be circumstances, however, in which additional stages are required. You should always make sure that the reviewer is quite clear about the number of drafting stages from the outset, otherwise the project is likely to run on, and on, and on.

The three-draft process is the method of ensuring that the quality both you and the owner require is obtained. Just how important the three shots at the target approach is to the overall success of the project will become apparent if we examine those two problems of assuredness and emotion in some detail.

8.1 The drafting stages

The first draft, developed from an understanding of the audience plus acknowledgement of the approved content of the synopsis and style guide and the support of the subject matter in the form of a computer system or standards and procedures, should fully and (fairly) accurately meet the objectives of the exercise. I think it should be possible to get at least 80 per cent of the book correct in the first draft. This sounds a high percentage, but you should remember that in a 100-page book this would mean that 20 pages are completely wrong!

Comments following presentation of the first draft will often be in the nature of 'you haven't understood how the system operates in this area', or 'this is not how we undertake this part of our work'. This is fine and the first draft review is the stage at which the gaps in your understanding can be filled.

In principle, the second draft should be a correction of the first draft. You will have submitted the first draft to the reviewer on hard copy, desktop published and including diagrams and examples of screens and printouts where appropriate. The first draft, duly marked up by the reviewer, will be used as input for the second draft.

The implication here is that the second draft should not contain any new material. In a perfect world this should be the case. You should only start to document a situation that is solid and stable. Unfortunately, this is not always possible and it is common for the second draft to contain up to 25 per cent of new material - text describing elements about which you had no knowledge when you wrote the first draft and that were not included in the synopsis. This situation is discussed in more detail later in this chapter.

Comments following presentation of the second draft - which should raise the book from being 80 per cent correct to 95 per cent correct - should be more in the nature of 'I don't think I can have explained this point to you properly' or the ever-gleeful 'I've found a spelling mistake!'

Once second draft comments have been incorporated, the final draft review should merely be a case of the reviewer checking that second draft comments have been included and no typographical errors have crept in.

Just as you should tell the reviewer at the outset about the number of draft stages the project is going to use, so you should also tell them what their expectations should be at each stage and allow them to reject it if it does not meet or at least approach those expectations.

8.2   Who should be involved in the draft review?

The reviewer must satisfy himself that your draft is well on the way to being perfect and that appropriate corrections are made and so he will take whatever steps are necessary for him to make a balanced judgement about your work. This might mean submitting the draft to the users themselves - who better, you might say, to check the accuracy of your text. Fair enough, but you can get too much of a good thing.

The introduction of a new hardware and software system in an organisation can be very sensitive, and the writing of the books can be used as a form of

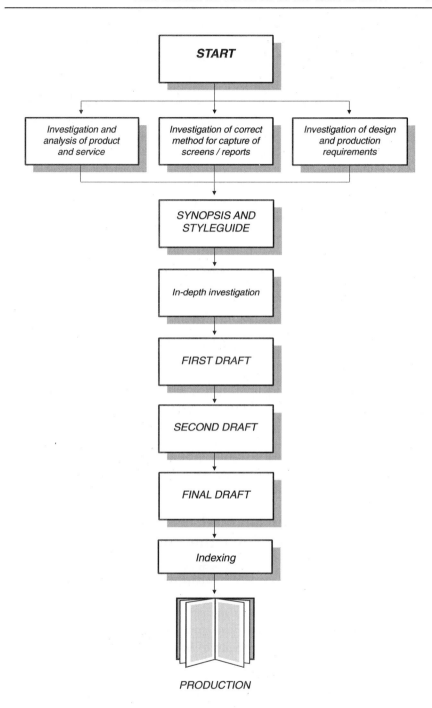

Figure 8.1
The project stages

red herring - to divert the attention of users from other difficulties arising during the implementation of the system. For me, this course of action was once taken to the limits of credibility when a colleague and I, the hapless writers, sat around a table with over thirty managers who represented the opinions of perhaps ten times that number. You will accept that every single person will probably have an opinion about documentation that varies at least slightly from that of his or her colleagues. How we ever got out of that one I will never know, but it did involve us in very considerable rewrites of text - to no measurable benefit either in our eyes or those of our main working contact.

So when your primary reviewer suggests that he may circulate the first draft to a number of other reviewers for their opinion, you must ensure that they fully understand the implications of doing this. There are likely to be two problems arising in this situation. The first is that unless all the reviewers are very disciplined about the time frame in which to conduct the review, it is likely to cause a delay in the project. The second is that reviewers may have conflicting views and receiving ten different marked-up drafts on which the comments disagree will not be a constructive way of proceeding to second draft.

I would recommend that you ask the primary reviewer to be the co-ordinator and arbitrator for this process. It will then be his or her responsibility to return a single marked-up draft incorporating all other reviewers' comments at an appropriate date. This will mean that if the primary reviewer has photocopied your first draft and given it to 823 people, it will be his or her job to collate the comments of 823 onto a single copy for your consideration. This usually has a sobering effect on the primary reviewer who will tend to let sweet reason prevail and at least keep the number of reviewers to a reasonable level.

Not that I like to discourage user participation at any stage in the process - such a course of action would be a complete negation of my principles - but such an exercise at the review stage can be very time consuming and costly and a balance between democracy and progress must be struck.

8.3   What sort of mark-up should you expect to receive from the reviewers?

The mark-up undertaken by the reviewer must be informative. While it might be good for the spleen to write 'NO!', 'RUBBISH!', 'THIS IS WRONG!', or even '****!' (expletive deleted) on a draft, these words only indicate some irritation on the part of the reviewer and tell you little of what is adrift. Such comments, and we have had them, are also insulting and forget that we are all supposedly on the same side, trying to help in the smooth installation or operation of a system or service.

Faced with this type of comment, I usually call a meeting with the graffiti artist and smile sweetly and innocently as I ask him quite where he wants me to insert the word '****'. This usually restores a level of professionalism to the meeting and the project in general.   But why should an otherwise reasonable person suddenly decide to rough-house someone who is only doing his best to earn a crust?

Show me a technical writer who claims that he has not been faced with this sort of problem, and I will either tell him he is a liar - or offer him a job. It is a curious phenomenon and I think I know why it happens. Many of us store up memories of a schoolteacher who rewarded the genuine and well-meant efforts of schoolday essay writing with just such a reaction. How dare he, we might have said, ridicule my work in such a humiliating way? How can he be so hurtful? I am not talking of experiences where, if we are fair, such a reaction was justified - we have all put in poor work and known full-well that it was well below par. But there have been times where we just misunderstood, or got the wrong end of the stick, and back it came with withering ·comments and a derisory mark out of ten.

Down into the subconscious it goes, waiting for an opportunity for revenge. Well, we never get back at the teacher in question - but the work of the technical author deliciously turns the tables and we can 'mark' the book just as that hated teacher did ... and we do. Red pen, which we want - so long as the comments are constructive - seems to raise a bloodlust in a small proportion of people and they go wild with the insults.

Don't worry about it if it happens. You can, however, try and pre-empt the situation by telling the reviewer how you want the text marked and why. Gently providing a reminder that you are not a mind reader, so this sort of comment is unhelpful, usually does the trick.

That's enough of the psychology, but one final note of warning.

From second to final draft should be something of a doddle. The content was accepted in the first draft, refined in the second, and now small design inconsistencies and verbal obfuscations will be picked up before final approval. Quite often, the reviewer/project manager may quietly show your final draft to the managing director or someone else up the line from themselves.

. This can be a good move, but often these people have not been party to the project, have not seen the synopsis, and have an in-built desire to 'mix it'. They may also have personal wishes and prejudices that do not really concern the mainstream if the project. On the whole and given the opportunity, it might be a good idea to suggest that our eager beaver keeps things to himself until the book is published.

8.4   Dealing with a system still under development

Documenting a system that is still under development or, even worse, still being specified, can present some difficulties. One way of solving the problem is to delay writing until the owner is sure that everything is ready for the writing task, but this may not be acceptable.

Another solution is to treat changes and additions as an amendment to the book - to be incorporated after acceptance of the final draft. This is rarely popular either, but it has a marvellously disciplining effect on the owner, who will positively rush through the drafts in order to get the new changes to the product documented.

Sometimes it is possible to add the new material at second draft stage, but you should be aware of the pitfalls when doing this. The first is, of course, that the reviewer treats the whole book as a first draft and expects two further draft stages to follow. The second follows from the first, that having incorporated new material and created a new first draft, a request is received to add further new material to this draft - this is a process that can continue *ad infinitum* if you are not very careful.

In this situation it is probably best to tie documentation production to the development stages for the system. If the developments at any stage mean that additional material has to be added to a book that has reached first draft, the synopsis should be formally changed and agreed, as should any additional draft stages required for that book as a consequence. This way everybody knows what is happening and what is expected of them.

8.5   Dealing with a change of reviewer

Essentially this is a similar problem to that of circulation to a number of reviewers or submission to a senior manager not hitherto involved.

Some people when taking over the control of the review side of the project are entirely reasonable, going along with previous decisions, even though they do not entirely agree with them. Others, however, will start to take things apart, finding fault with the synopsis, the style, and drafts already agreed. This is a difficult situation to handle and will again involve telling the new reviewer of the cost and time implications of what they are suggesting. How hard you argue your case when the new person is adamant despite all other considerations will have to depend on whether you believe their suggestions will make a real improvement and contribution to the project.

9 Some guidelines for producing effective text

Before we start to discuss the writing process in detail, let me state the obvious. Naturally you should only write using a computer with a word-processing package. To try to write anything that is going to be edited heavily without using modern technology will add significantly to your workload, so the days of writing technical documentation in longhand are very definitely over.

In our case, as we normally desktop publish our books, we need to use a package that is compatible with our chosen desktop publishing system. If we are producing a book that incorporates scientific symbols, we must ensure that the products we use provide this capability. These are really the only constraints, unless you are a contractor, in which case some further restrictions may be imposed by the owner. Most organisations that have the courage to subcontract their writing to a third party want to keep some degree of control over the situation, so they will insist upon the writer using a word-processing package that is known to them. This can mean buying a copy of a package and, horror of horrors, having to learn a new system. There are, fortunately, ways of converting text from one system to another, so I, at least, am spared the ignominy of having to do some nail-biting homework.

9.1 What tools do I need?

I tend to rely on two outside sources other than my notes concerning the job in question. The first is a good dictionary - Collins or Chambers are both excellent. I do not use these to find wonderfully obscure words, but to ensure that I use words correctly. If I don't, the precision I desire may be lost and with it the clear understanding that I hope to achieve from my audience. You may find it curious that someone who earns his living from writing admits to using a dictionary for such a fundamental purpose, but there it is.

The other 'prop' I use is a synonym dictionary. Synonyms, for those who are unfamiliar with the word, are 'like meanings'. Of course English is such a rich language that, in a sense, there are no synonyms at all - every word has its own unique meaning or nuance. However, when you are writing about a precise and rather narrow topic, it is very useful to be able to sharpen up the text by using different words, even if that means risking a slight broadening of the reader's perception.

9.2   Starting to write

So, now are you ready to write?

Well, perhaps.

Let us assume the following:

- you have the signed-off synopsis and you are satisfied that the reviewer has a clear idea of what he or she is getting.
- you have looked at the computer system and at least know where to look for further information as it is required.
- you have studied the audience in detail and you know about what they will tolerate in terms of style and length. You also know what their job is about and how much pressure they are under.

If these elements are all in place, you may begin to write.

But where do you start?

Are you quite sure that you can transport yourself inside the head of your reader - seeing the process you intend to document from his perspective, or do you feel just a little uncertain about some of the detail? Remembering your avowed intention to write in a style that is neither patronising nor over the heads of your audience, can you visualise how the words should come out on the page? Do you, in short, feel comfortable about commencing, or are you reluctant to write?

Temperament also has its fearful part to play. At the risk of becoming extremely precious about the writing process, writing is an extension of your personality - your soul even. It is, therefore, much more 'driven' by what kind of a person you are and how you feel on the day than, say, being an accountant or a bus driver. No, I'm not saying that an accountant's or a bus driver's performance is not affected by how they feel on a particular day. On an off day, an accountant will make mistakes, but he will still account. On an off day, a bus driver will jolt the dentures of the old age pensioners and scare the living daylights out of innocent motorcyclists, but he will still drive. When a writer is feeling unproductive, however, it might be far better for mankind in general and his employer in particular if he just took the day off and spent the time in usefully lifting a row of potatoes. A little later in this chapter you will find some suggestions showing how my colleagues and I try to overcome this problem.

But where do you start?

The synopsis is the first straw (or quill?) to the drowning author.

This will have given your reviewer a clear view of what you wanted to write at the time. You will, of course, have done some further investigation since the synopsis was submitted and hopefully it will still be accurate. If, as a result of your further research, you are no longer satisfied with the structure or content of the documents you wanted to write, you must alter the synopsis and resubmit it for approval.

But let's just assume that your surveys and procrastinations have done little to alter your objectives as set out in the synopsis. You must now start to write and, one would assume, this means sitting at the keyboard of a PC and conjuring up some words.

I must confess to feeling a little daunted at the start of a writing exercise. On the negative side, I have some considerable forces lined up against me. I have the constraints and disciplines of the synopsis and the styleguide. I have a clear view of the capabilities and inclinations of my audience - but they are many and varied. And I have a fair view of what the system will do. This, of course, implies that I also have a fair view of what the system will NOT do and what must be addressed by describing manual systems.

On the positive side, I know that there are a number of useful arrows in my quiver. The first of these is my ability to go back to any aspect that I want to revisit throughout the project. It is very important that the writer maintains a positive relationship with all his contacts throughout the process. Talking to the reviewer, the audience or end-users, the software development people, the standards officers - whoever is involved - benefits both parties. The writer provides progress reports - always an important thing for the reviewer or controller of the project who can be a little unnerved by the fact that there is remarkably little to see for a long period at the beginning of the writing process. The writer, in return, should be receiving up-to-the-minute intelligence about changes that may be taking place within the system development process - both the detail of the system and the implementation schedule.

The second point making me feel more positive is the security one gains from the presence of the editorial process - discussed in detail later in this book. Without this, there is no critique of your work until it is seen by the reviewer - and that is far too risky for all but the most confident of writers.

The third is the business of developing three drafts. This does not mean that the writer will be writing the book three times, as explained in a previous chapter. In fact, the three draft process should reduce the amount of actual writing done, as it strictly controls the writing process from all points of view.

9.3   Writing style

You have already seen some general considerations about writing style in the synopsis chapter. This section provides some further detail on this subject. Although, as I said at the start of the book, this is not a grammar reference, I will touch upon this now and again where I consider it significant.

9.3.1   Choosing your words

It is very important that the text remains bright, light, and interesting and this can be difficult where there is a considerable amount of repetition - for example, where menu options are being used to explain a business function. Intelligent use of good dictionaries - both English and synonym - will do much to improve the quality of the text you prepare.

For example, you may find yourself writing about a stock control system. After a while, the use of the word 'stock' will start to grate in your mind and if this is something you notice, you can be sure that the reader will notice it too. My synonym dictionary provides literally dozens of variations on a theme of stock held under a total of eighteen sub-headings. The most appropriate to our definition of 'stock' are:

inventory	*supply*	*lot*	*load*
collection	*aggregate*	*reserve*	*hoard*
range	*goods*	*produce*	*commodities*
products	*items*	*articles*	*stock in trade*
merchandise	*vendibles*	*material*	*resource*

Clearly, some of these words alter the meaning we want to convey too much. For instance, the generally accepted meaning of 'aggregate' has tended to move on from a collective role to describe multi-mineral rocks, or plain old sand and gravel. Clearly, to talk about 'aggregated raw materials' when meaning all raw materials collected together in one place would make many think in terms of minerals only - and a rather restricted range of minerals at that.

Similarly, vendibles are stock items for sale - and not all stock is sold in its present stocked state. For example, welding rods held in the warehouse stock of an engineering company will rarely be sold, but will be used in the process of fusing two or more pieces of metal together.

However, using products, stock in trade, goods, inventory, and merchandise as a light relief from the endless repetition of the word 'stock' will improve your text enormously. If you want to see if you have fallen into a situation of word overpopulation, try reading a suspect passage aloud. Very quickly you will see where the problems arise.

As a general principle, technical terms should be avoided at all costs. All specialist subjects, computing particularly, have a bewildering argot of their own and this usually comes about as a manifestation of one of the worst human failings. Man has a terrible tendency to try to elevate himself by appearing to be of superior intellect, and one way seems to be to invent new words that are calculated to prove confusing to the man in the street. Worse, some words are used quite incorrectly with the same general result.

Although using the word 'bug' to indicate a fault in a program has a nice piece of recent folklore surrounding its invention, error would be a much better word which everyone would understand. Things, however, have become much worse in the ensuing years since the arrival of the bug, with new words for practically every concept and the twisting of hitherto respected words to complicate the situation further. Witness database, useability, interface, invoke, and many, many more.

So, use words that everyone can understand, but technical terms you cannot avoid using should appear in the glossary.

9.3.2   *Keeping the text short and readable*

Where possible, I replace as many words as I can with symbols and a careful 'bullet-point' structure. The fewer the words, the more the book will be read. This business of replacing words wherever possible has been discussed elsewhere, but it cannot be overstressed. Often companies have fallen down on the job of developing documentation simply because they have tried to do too much. If they had concentrated on giving the reader what he or she needed, rather than attempting to explain every possible aspect, they might have completed the job long before we were invited, in desperation, to become involved.

Please remember, producing your words in the context of the impression you gained from your future readership has nothing to do with drawing disparaging conclusions about the audience's intellect. You cannot judge the intelligence or brain capacity of someone by the things they read when they are relaxing. Nor should you - you are here to inform, not educate, confuse, or depress. If, after reading your book, they do not understand what they should know, it is your fault, not theirs. The success of your work and the measure of a good writer of user documentation are the contribution you make to the overall success of the project and system. Was it installed quickly? Did you reduce the incidence of unnecessary calls to the help desk? Were the users confident? Was the system used fully, accurately, and intelligently? If these things are not achieved, you will have failed.

To take an extreme example, if the *Mr. Men* books for children were not so charmingly illustrated, with words that appealed to children and little hidden ironies that make them a pleasure for parents to read out aloud, they would not have been a success. Whose fault would that have been? The parents'? The children's? No, the author's. But they are a success - a resounding success and a beacon to us all.

This aspect of your work is about inclination, not intellect. And you as the writer cannot hope to educate - to train - your audience by some ill-conceived notion of lifting them onto a higher intellectual plane. Megalomaniacs are not required in the ranks of writers. You can only hope to inform, interest, enthuse.

9.3.3   Using symbols and illustrations

Symbols can be invaluable in helping to reduce the amount of text you are required to write, making the page more appealing to the reader. Of course, the use of symbols and decisions regarding which elements you are going to explain in detail and which you are going to leave to the reader's imagination must be explained very carefully. There is no point in introducing whizzy writing techniques and bewildering symbols if you do not, at the very least, supply a key.

Screen and report examples can often prove useful as illustrations. Screen prints not only allow the reader to see the text in context when reading away from the screen, but also allow a reader at the screen to be sure that they are in the right place. Similarly, report illustrations with annotation can make a report description much clearer.

You should use diagrams judiciously. Although they can lighten the text enormously, they should be used to further explain a detail or to replace text. You should never incorporate a diagram for its own sake with no particular relevance to the subject matter being discussed.

The next three illustrations (Figures 9.1 - 9.3) show examples of different types of books and the way in which symbols have been used to lift the text.

These examples all illustrate the setting up of a simple piece of information. However, you will see that the first example is very text heavy, whereas the other two are much lighter to read. The last of the examples assumes a reader with a fairly high level of knowledge and therefore leaves out the screen illustration and descriptions of key depressions, the principles of which would have been described to the reader earlier in the book.

9.3.4   Maintaining a consistent style

This is partly concerned with layout and partly a matter of how the book is written. If the synopsis insists on a book written in the second person, it is very easy to slip into a passive third person occasionally.

Figure 9.1
A simple but wordy
book

MAINTAINING RECORDS
OF PAYMENT TERMS

Descriptions of the various types of payment terms that may be applied to customers must be kept on the system. These will be used by the RCL system when calculating the due dates for invoices. These records may be added to, changed, or deleted as follows:

- from the Main Menu, select option 10

- from the File Maintenance Menu, select option 4

- from the General Information Menu, select option 9 - Payment Terms

The following screen will appear:

Figure 3.8
The file should
contain a
description of
each set of
payment terms.

```
Test System
GH02936              Maintain Payment Terms           CHANGE
21/01/93
  Payment Terms __

Type options, press Enter

?  Payment       Description          Credit    Credit
   Terms                              From      Days
   H1            Draft with order       I         0
   H2            Cheque at Delivery     I         0
   H3            Draft at Delivery      I         0
   H4            Credit                 M        30
   H5            Invoice Direct Debit   I         0




F3=Exit    F10 - Delete
```

Payment Terms Enter the code identifying the set of payment terms. This field is mandatory.

Description Enter a description of these payment terms.

Credit From Enter I if the due date is calculated from the invoice date. Enter M if the due date is calculated from the end of the month in which the invoice is produced. This field is mandatory.

Credit Days Enter the number of days to be added to the Credit From date when calculating the due date for an invoice. This field is mandatory.

If you do not wish to update the system with your changes, press F3. To switch between Add mode and Change mode, press F9. When the details have been entered correctly, press the Enter key to update the system. If you wish to delete a record of a payment type, key D in the ? selection column and then press F10.

Figure 9.2
Raising the interest
by using illustration

SECTION 10 **PAYMENT TERMS**

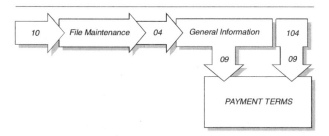

You may create codes that identify the different payment terms that you allow your customers. The RCL system uses these payment terms when calculating the due dates for invoices. When you select this option, the following screen will be displayed:

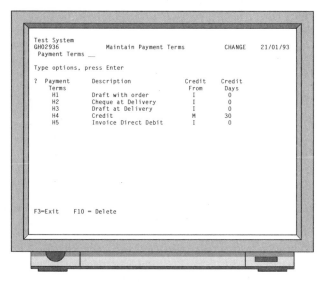

```
Test System
GH02936              Maintain Payment Terms           CHANGE    21/01/93
 Payment Terms __

Type options, press Enter

? Payment       Description              Credit   Credit
  Terms                                  From     Days
  H1            Draft with order         I        0
  H2            Cheque at Delivery       I        0
  H3            Draft at Delivery        I        0
  H4            Credit                   M        30
  H5            Invoice Direct Debit     I        0




F3=Exit    F10 = Delete
```

 Payment Terms
Credit From
Credit Days

CREDIT FROM   I - if the due date is calculated from the invoice date.
M - if the due date is calculated from the end of the month in which the invoice is produced.

 To switch between Add mode and Change mode.

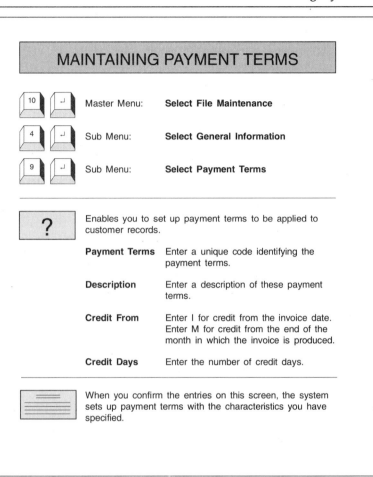

Figure 9.3
Minimising the words
to provide a quick
and easy read

For example, 'When the screen is displayed', rather than 'when you display the screen' has a nasty habit of rearing its ugly head.

As the task is to inform, the user documentation should not be used for flights of creative fancy. For the repetitive parts of the manual, you should always keep in a low-key consistent mode of writing. If you use the phrase, 'you complete the screen as follows', you should not try to ring the changes by saying 'you do the following' or any other variation. The introductory chapters are the only places where it is laudable to wax lyrical.

9.4   The front matter

I have already mentioned what I call 'front matter' and this needs to be handled professionally if the right impression is to be conveyed to the reader.

To repeat, front matter will contain some or all of the following:

- a copyright notice, complete with the © copyright mark
- a statement about copyright
- a liability notice
- a warranty notice
- acknowledgement for the use of trademarks in the document
- a by-line
- a thank-you to those who helped the writers in their task
- the name and address of the owner's company
- the ISBN number, if the book is being published in the 'real' sense
- a version number of the document and, if appropriate, any associated software package's version number
- a welcome message or preface
- a contents sheet.

When describing the synopsis, we outlined the reasons for the inclusion of some of these items. For some of them the wording or appearance is quite critical and these are described below.

9.4.1   The copyright statement and notice

The copyright statement **must** be in the following format:

Copyright © PALL-OT Systems Limited 1993.

or:

© PALL-OT Systems Limited 1993.

To this you may add a statement about reproduction restrictions. This statement is usually couched in legalistic terms and indeed many writers work for organisations that have already developed their own terminology to cover these eventualities. A typical example will contain the following warnings:

All rights reserved. You may not reproduce, transmit, transcribe, store in a retrieval system, or translate into any language or computer language, in any form or by any means, electronic, mechanical, optical, chemical, manual, or otherwise, any part of this publication without the express written permission of PALL-OT Systems Limited.

You should note that if the book is to be published in different countries, there may be specific requirements for the wording in these countries.

9.4.2   The liability notice

In the chapter describing the contents of a synopsis, it was explained that responsibility for the interpretation and use of a computer system or service is, on the whole, not a good thing to have! This being the case, most documentation contains a liability notice even where the system or service is only going to be used 'internally'.

Most liability notices contain the following message:

> *Every effort has been made to ensure that the Real-time Corporate Logistics (RCL) system supplied by PALL-OT Systems Limited is described accurately and completely in this and other associated documentation. However, as use and interpretation of the RCL system and the associated support documentation is beyond the control of the PALL-OT Systems Limited, no liability, either direct or consequential, can be entertained by PALL-OT Systems Limited, its agents, or its suppliers.*

The important things to note are the ' ... or consequential' and the term 'suppliers'.

Consequential loss is a real problem. A company might argue that its computer system caused it to have to call in the receivers, if the error was concerned with interpretation of the accounts. It could argue that, as a consequence of the information not being clear, it made decisions that were subsequently found to be wrong. These wrong decisions, they might argue, tumbled the company. So the actual loss was minimal - time wasted on looking at an inaccurate report, perhaps. The consequential loss, however, could run into millions.

9.4.3   The warranty notice

The warranty notice further protects the owner and writer. The following is an example:

> *No warranty, whether expressed or implied, is offered concerning the accuracy of this or any other associated documentation, or for the features, applicability, or appropriateness of the Real-time Corporate Logistics system described herein.*

Now, there are laws about not being able to wriggle out of everything one does. Responsibility cannot entirely be shed by the inclusion of clever legalistic wording in the frontispiece. However, the inclusion of these clauses should protect a company in the event of misuse of documentation, unless the conduct of the writing project was careless and sloppy, giving rise to widespread and material errors in the text.

9.4.4   Trademarks

If your book contains names that are registered trademarks belonging to other organisations, you must ensure that they are either flagged by the appropriate trademark symbol every time they occur or mentioned at the beginning of the book. So:

> *Real-time Corporate Logistics and RCL are registered trademarks of PALL-OT Systems Limited of Guiseley, West Yorkshire.*

9.4.5   The welcome message or preface

The choice between a welcome message and a preface is sometimes an emotional one.

A welcome message may appear in the first chapter or it may form a part of the front matter. The wording is often a bit of a selling exercise on the books and the system or service that it claims to explain. It can inform the reader about where to look for certain pieces of information and it may provide information about support beyond the books. This might mean details, including a phone number, for a help desk in a large organisation.

At the end of reading the welcome section - never more than a single page if you want it to be read - the reader should feel confidence in themselves and in the fact that the book is going to be enormously supportive in the overall learning process. If you want an everyday example of a good welcome section in another context, think of the leaflets handed out at theme parks, country houses, and some of the larger museums. Without giving anything away - the proper guidebook costing lots of money does that - it shows the layout of the site, the restaurants, the toilets, facilities for the disabled, and any landmarks. This is in effect what you should achieve in the welcome message - a signpost to what is to come and an answering of half-asked, basic questions.

Alternatively, you may want to use a short, matter of fact preface, getting over the basic points but without being too gushing. As with everything in the process, the choice will be determined, at least in part, by your readership. My colleagues, a hard-headed lot, claim that they would be completely switched off by a welcome message, but would consider reading a preface. Others, maybe those more nervous of approaching a system and its documentation, may require the encouragement and reassurance of the welcome message.

9.4.6   The contents sheet

The contents sheet seems to present some authors with a real problem. They seem to either dismiss it as worthless, in which case it becomes nothing more than a chapter list, or it runs to 12 or more pages with lines of explanation as to the contents - rather in the manner of a Victorian novel. For example, 'Chapter the Third, in which there is a secret tryst in the forest which is frustrated by the absence of one party, and only the horse derives any lasting pleasure' (a small prize for the first person who recognises the poem being referred to here).

It has been said that readers of a technical manual will look for a documented solution to their problem for about 40 seconds. After this time, they will abandon the job, ask someone else, or try on their own. We have, therefore, 40 seconds for readers to translate their question into our terminology and then find what they are looking for.

Rapid access to information is the key to success, and the contents sheet gives us a great opportunity to provide some good clues as to the whereabouts of the information.

To a certain extent, the contents sheet is driven by the structure of the book. If the book is task driven, the chapter and section titles should be self-explanatory. You may wish to show details to sub-section level here, but beware of the list getting too long.

The only other consideration will be whether to show page numbers. This will depend on the pagination method you have chosen. If you are paginating within numbered sections, it may be perfectly acceptable to provide a contents list in the format shown below in Figure 9.4.

In this case, each section will start a new page one with the change of section number, and will be easily identifiable. If you have paginated sequentially or within chapter, however, and maybe only refer to sections by name, you will need to include the page numbers (Figure 9.5).

Chapter 1	Introduction	
Chapter 2	Overview	
Chapter 3	Entering orders for credit sales	
	3/1	Enter orders for non-trade customers
	3/2	Enter orders for trade customers
	3/3	Add new products to a customer product list
	3/4	Negotiate prices
	3/5	View stock availability details
	3/6	View delivery availability details
Chapter 4	Entering orders for cash sales	
	4/1	Enter cash sale orders
	4/2	Negotiate prices
	4/3	View stock availability details
	4/4	View delivery availability details

Figure 9.4
Contents lists for chapters with numbered sections

Figure 9.5
Contents lists for
chapters with unnumbered
sections

Chapter 1   Introduction 1-1

Chapter 2   Overview 2-1

Chapter 3   Entering orders for credit sales
            Enter orders for non-trade customers 3-1
            Enter orders for trade customers 3-6
            Add new products to a customer product list 3-12
            Negotiate prices 3-15
            View stock availability details 3-19
            View delivery availability details 3-20

Chapter 4   Entering orders for cash sales
            Enter cash sale orders 4-1
            Negotiate prices 4-6
            View stock availability details 4-7
            View delivery availability details 4-9

9.5   The end matter

Most books are concluded by three possible elements - a glossary of terms, an index, and one or more appendices.

9.5.1   *The glossary*

Glossaries are included to explain the technical terms used in the document and to provide an element of discipline where several terms are used in an organisation to mean one thing (see Figure 9.6).

So where possible use words that everyone can understand, but contentious words you cannot avoid using should appear in the glossary. Light, supportive explanations should accompany the entry and, needless to say, the glossary should be in alphabetical order. To make things easy for yourself, do not try to cross-reference words in the glossary from the text, or provide page references back into the text from the glossary. This will make maintenance of the books a nightmare and it is simply not necessary.

9.5.2   *The index*

The index can prove another stumbling block to the uninitiated, but indexes are really quite easy to construct and can provide the writer with another opportunity to scan through his or her work and identify errors that might otherwise go unnoticed.

There is a professional body of indexers and they have some weird and wonderful methods for indexing that result in real Rolls-Royce products. My own

Figure 9.6
Glossary example

GLOSSARY

Backup	The process by which a copy of the information on your computer system is made.
BCR	Business Control Report.
Buying Group	A number of customers from one or more companies that have formed a group in order to obtain special buying prices for your products.
Class of Trade	A means of classifying the different types of customer you supply.
CMD	Credit Management Department.
Communications Link	A physical link between a device and a computer that allows them to communicate with one another.
Contact History	A record of letters and other contacts made with a customer by the accounts department.
Delivery Area	A part of the total geographical area in which you supply products. This is used as a guide to despatchers.
Direct Debit	A means by which payments can be requested directly from customers bank account through the bank clearing system.
EFT	Electronic Funds Transfer.
Mnemonic	A code name for something that is made up in such a way a to give a good indication of the full name. RCL uses two types of mnemonic. One to identify customers, and one to identify products.

view is that, just as our readership enjoy simple text and diagrams, they benefit from a simple and clear approach to the business of indexing.

The purpose of an index is to enable the reader to find the location of something at topic level. This means that it is far more detailed than the contents sheet. Once again, however, there is a fine line between providing too little - in which case it is little more use than the contents sheet at the other end of the book - and too much, in which case far too high a portion of that 40 second span of enquiry available to us will be eaten up in a frustrating and ultimately fruitless search.

My view is that indexes can either be for the book in question, or they can be for several different volumes if together they provide a collective description of a business operation or computer system. If the latter course is adopted, the index will be inserted in all of the companion volumes.

In the following example (Figure 9.7), the 'combined' index is adopted and the first part of the reference refers to the book, which might in this case be Order Processing, Despatch, Stores, or Set-up and Maintenance. The entries in

Figure 9.7
A multi-level index

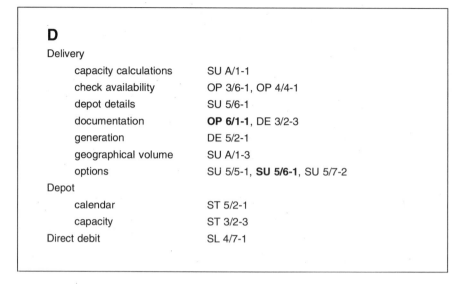

bold type show where the most comprehensive information concerning the topic is to be found. This is particularly welcome where more than one book is involved and the reader needs to know that he is at least thumbing through the right volume! The balance of the reference shows a chapter, section, and page number within section, manual structure.

When providing an index that runs across books like this, you must ensure that you include a key to the book codes!

You will notice a number of things about the small example shown on the previous page. The first is the use of two levels of entry in the index - the main entry (Delivery, Depot, Direct debit) and the sub-entry (depot details and documentation within Delivery). Two levels are really the maximum for the kind of documentation we are preparing. The second point you should notice is the use of emboldening to identify the main reference for a topic, which has already been mentioned.

There are several instances where two quite separate indexes may be needed. If the book is task driven there may be a need to cross-reference tasks with screen options and one way of handling this is to have an index devoted to providing a 'translation' to business objective and screen. There are other instances and the best way of handling these is to stand back from what you have written when it is complete and ask yourself honestly if you feel readers will be able to find what they are looking for, wherever they are coming from.

Indexing is where I throw away the technology altogether and return to manual methods of a curiously Heath-Robinson level of sophistication.

I am aware of the fact that there are all sorts of clever computing devices to identify all references to this word or that word-string, and that I could generate indexes automatically. Indeed, some of the word-processing and desktop publishing products carry out this sort of work. But I am indexing a book, trying to identify the best sources of information for my reader. No computer yet devised can differentiate between the use of a word where it is incidental to the text and where it is of vital importance.

For example, if the subject of the book is a CASE product, the word 'CASE' will appear hundreds of times in the text. There will, however, be a number of specific areas where essential information is available. Often these will appear as sub-entries just like the example shown above. The benefit of sub-entries is that one can include a reference in the context of some other topic or activity. For example, you might have as a sub-entry the analysis stage within CASE, or the login window associated with CASE, the strategy stage of CASE, etc. In this way your index is becoming very useful to the reader.

Nor can a computer identify where I might wish something to appear twice in the index under different titles, e.g. stock item and product. This is not to say the computerised indexing does not have its place. You may, once you have identified the words to be indexed and their locations, wish to identify these permanently through your system so that future reindexing is made easier.

Now to the world of Heath-Robinson - he of the crazy cartoons with golfers swinging nibbletts spliced with knotted string, and ancient steam locomotives with unlikely birds nesting in tall chimneys. To index a book, I take 26 sheets of paper, put them in a binder, and head them up A through to Z with a biro. I then start to read my book with an indexer's eye. When I reach an entry of import, it goes into my binder under the appropriate letter. Where sub-entries seem to contribute positively to the clarification of the point, I also write these in.

Gradually a picture begins to take shape and my pieces of paper become ever more scribbled on. Some references I will ignore as they obviously either repeat something that has already gone before or they say nothing that is of real value to the reader. When the book has been read right through to the end, I will sort the entries under each letter into alphabetical order and key them all into a word processor. *Voilà*, an index.

Some of my compatriots will be completely mystified at my use of paper and pen. Although they use a similar constructional technique, they tend to do it all on a word-processor, inserting new entries in sequence as they go. I can only assume that my attachment to the basics dates back to a time when I lived in the north of England and used the time spent on frequent train journeys to London for such tasks as indexing. In those days portable PCs were not yet invented.

Naturally, because of the page references, the index cannot be prepared until after the final draft of the book has been signed off. Often the users and owners have to be advised of the reasons for the non-availability of the index almost at the beginning of the exercise, but to do it at first draft stage would be to add exponentially to the work.

9.5.3   Appendices

I am not keen on Appendices.

Why?

Because they are hardly ever read.

Sometimes it is difficult to see how they can be avoided. Some documents require the inclusion of legal wording, sample forms, lists of codes and definitions, or some other reference material, and the easy option is to throw them all in a big heap at the back, call them Appendix 1, Appendix 2, and so on, and then put as informative an entry in the contents sheet as possible.

But it is all a bit of a waste of time if they won't be read.

If you think about my comment concerning the 'selfish read' aspect of user documentation, a selfish read is also a lazy read. Your text should provide a one-stop-shop for everything the reader needs, and if you have to include a text line which says, 'full details of this aspect may be found in Appendix 14', you may be sure your reader will read your words, but not refer to the appendix.

The best way is to include everything the reader may want to know in a single source, signposted by entries in the contents sheet and the index, and leave out any unnecessary padding. If your book refers to the *Maastricht Agreement*, let them go and find a copy of their own, rather than including it in all its glory in the appendices.

The only time I am comfortable with an appendix is where the book includes a number of forms used for input of information which the user should photocopy each time they are needed. Even then, I try to avoid calling it an appendix - what is wrong with 'sample forms' as a chapter in the book? As most manuals are bound in loose-leaf binders, the actual location from which the forms are taken for photocopying purposes is largely irrelevant. In fact, there is an argument for including them in the body of the book rather than at the end, as there is always a tendency for the last page to become a little dog-eared. This will be particularly so where the last page has to be removed fairly regularly.

You have to use your personal judgement on this matter, but remember never to include any information of vital importance in an appendix because it may never be read.

9.6   Personal editing

Personal editing is an important aspect of the writer's work and not to be confused with the process described in the next chapter of this book. The conscientious author will carry out two levels of personal editing.

A preliminary edit is a necessary first stage, but the most important personal edit takes place with the writer a long way from the PC.

A quick word about the preliminary editing stage first. I carry this out on the screen, although some of my colleagues have to see the printed page to perform any kind of edit. I edit at two levels on the screen - one for grammatical sense and flow and the other for spelling.

The first is about making sure that the sentences are constructed properly and that the ideas seem to progress logically from one to another. You will be surprised to see how much confusion there is in your words owing to poor punctuation. What seemed perfectly clear when you keyed it in is now confusing and requires two or three reads before it seems to make any sense. I hope that as few professional writers as possible subscribe to the modern theory that all punctuation is bad and that the fewer the full stops, commas, etc., the better.

New paragraphs have a wonderful effect on the reader, too. They slow up the absorption rate and give the writer an opportunity to move the subject matter on in a clear and understandable way. Much of my on-screen editing is about punctuation and paragraphing and it all comes about because I am actually reading my text.

The second on-screen check is fortunately supported by a spell-checker, which is a marvellous idea only marred by two limitations. The first is the fact that the spell-checker I use was obviously originally developed in the USA, so in some instances it rejects English spellings and passes the American ones. Spell-checkers are, like everything else, getting much better these days but this is still something to watch out for.

The second is, of course, that it is a spell-checker only and therefore is unable to differentiate between words spelled wrongly in context but nonetheless accurate words for all that. Thus, on and won, there and their, wring and writing, fore and four and for, files and flies, all get through. So, in some spell-checkers, do those unfortunate repetitions that seem to creep into the the text when we least expect them. But then, picking up these types of errors is the editor's job, isn't it?

You should also beware of plunking away at the 'overlook' key during the spell-checker correction process in a half-comatose state of mind. There is really no excuse for including genuinely misspelled words in your text. It is human to err, but inhuman to mischeck.

When you are happy with the grammar and the story you are gleaning from the screen, you should print the book out onto some scrap paper and leave it for a day or two.

When you have safely forgotten the detail of the book, go away to somewhere calm and peaceful. Before you start to read, try to put yourself back into the position of the audience. Remember their work and their workload. Remember the pressure or lack of it. Think of the photographs of the children, the family dog, the loved one. Think of the reading material lying in the office or workplace - was it *Pride and Prejudice*, or a puzzle book? And then read your book.

Remember the things you were trying to avoid when you were writing:

- making great leaps of assumption about the knowledge of the reader
- using abbreviations and acronyms without explaining them
- using technical jargon
- varying your style of writing
- structuring the text badly so that it does not flow
- using long and unwieldy sentences
- using ambiguous sentences
- using inappropriate illustrations
- providing too little detail so the text will not be informative and helpful
- providing too much detail so that the text becomes turgid and uninteresting
- changing the terminology you have used.

Do the words in your document achieve their goal and avoid these pitfalls? You must decide. If they do, go on to the hoop of fire discussed in the next chapter, for your editor will decide if your book passes muster - if he is a good editor. If they do not, try to decide which element of the task you have failed to address properly and carry out a correction. Then go on, and read on.

9.7   Dealing with writer's block

There are some writers who can isolate themselves from themselves and just turn out the same quality of work whatever, while others are more temperamental - producing brilliant work when they are at their best, but not able to keep the quality up all of the time.

All writers have their own way of working, but my own approach is to set-up a file on my PC for every chapter. Having set out all my files, I have, in a sense, mapped out my canvas. Many artists do not start with mixing oils and daubing, but put down a rough sketch of their picture with a pencil or charcoal. To a professional writer, setting up the chapter files is a similar process - roughly sketching in the basic outline of the work before filling in the details.

Writers often argue that starting work on a new book is pure agony. I do not suffer from this problem, but part of the reason might be the discipline of file set-up and development of the front matter. It 'gets you going' without much brain work being required.

This approach has another positive advantage. The nature of the chapters in the book varies considerably. Some chapters are fairly mindless stuff - just churning through the business objective and documenting the operation of the system within the context of those objectives. Others - introductions, lists of questions, job descriptions, overviews, glossaries, indexes - require a great deal more thought and care. Depending on the writer's mood, therefore, it is possible to move around the book like an artist moves about his canvas - concentrating on the broad picture here or paying enormous attention to detail there. From this you will deduce that it is not necessary to think in terms of writing a business or technical document from beginning to end in strict chronological order.

Beyond these two aids, there is nothing to do but to start writing. While I will admit to off-days when I just cannot seem to set down anything worthy of reading by anyone and must, therefore, reluctantly sympathise with others who also suffer from 'writer's block', there is a need for a degree of ruthlessness. Writing may be an art form in certain situations, but writers of user documentation are tradesmen. The writing process in the context of documenting business situations is a manufactory. It is necessary, therefore, just to get on with it and rely on the editing process (both personal and external, as described in the next chapter) to improve on poor quality when it appears once in a while.

9.8   Productivity

So, how much should you write in a day?

In terms of providing budgets - in other words statistics for consumption - you should reckon on no more than 2,000 words a day from the moment you start work, post-acceptance of the synopsis and styleguide, to presentation of the first draft. Although this is double the target most writers of fiction would expect to achieve, it should still allow plenty of time for progress meetings, further little sorties into the world of the detective, off-days, your own personal editing and redrafting, and desktop publishing.

Most technical authors must, therefore, count on writing a great deal more than 2,000 words a day in order to absorb the additional tasks described above. Many can put down anything up to 15,000 words in a day, but will still only achieve a 2,000 a day mean average. So the work is very varied - one day throwing words onto the page in the manner of a modern artist scattering and spattering in seemingly gay and prolific abandon - while another day is spent refining and thinking, with little demonstrable progress but a great deal actually being achieved.

10 Editing - the vitally necessary evil

What is an editor? One dictionary has it that an editor is 'a person in overall charge of the editing and often the policy of a newspaper or periodical'. This goes well beyond simple correction of text and I think this definition is more appropriate to the task of technical writing than the obvious role of simply reading and correcting text. The editor in the technical and user guide environment has a very great many things to check, and unless he holds a position of project management and perhaps even benign superiority on the project, there will be very little chance of a corporate book being produced. The editor is, therefore, a crucial part of the writing team.

The main benefit of involving an editor is to have another pair of eyes or, as you will read, more than one other pair of eyes, to read the book and iron out the errors and omissions. The editor also fulfils another very important role which is the identification and elimination of an individual's personal writing traits and whimsy, which can become very irritating to the reader. If there is no editor, these faults will slip through to the reviewer or user of the book with potentially disastrous consequences for the image and credibility of the writer.

If we accept the value of an editor for the above reasons, but restrict his role to one of 'suggester', his comments might not be considered until the development of the next draft or, more likely, they will be completely ignored. It is, therefore, necessary to give the editor a degree of clout for the editing process to be of lasting benefit to the project as a whole.

10.1 Background to the editing task

The books written to describe computer or business functions are written within the context of, as it were, several 'policies'. That of the owner, that of the reviewer, and that of the technical writing team or contractor(s) providing the documentation.

The owner may already have clearly defined standards for writing style and presentation. The reviewer will also have some ideas about what he hopes to achieve from professionally produced documentation. The views of both the owner and reviewer should have been made abundantly clear to the writer during the period leading up to the survey and synopsis stages. The writers will also have policies and these should have been firmly stated in the synopsis.

The policies finally adopted for the project will, therefore, be complex and varied. They will not only be concerned with writing style and presentation, but will also address the methodology to be adopted and the kind of books to be written.

These policies must be in the mind of the editor when he starts to work on a book. I say editor, but there may be two or even more editors because there is a lot to do and many things have to happen before a book is in a fit state to be presented for review.

As you will have read, a three-draft process is recommended, so the submission of a first draft is by no means the end of the story - there are other opportunities to get it right. However, the book should be well on the right lines before it is sent to the reviewer at first draft stage, because the second and third drafts should be concerned with improving the first draft and not a completely new exercise.

So what are we editing?

Essentially we are performing an internal check on the quality of a book before it is passed outside the writing team to the reviewer. Every book must meet the following quality standards before its first draft is released for external consumption:

- the book conforms to any design and stylistic requirements set by the owner and reviewer
- the text is syntactically correct
- the ideas flow logically throughout the book
- the structure and content conform to the synopsis
- the text and layout conform to the styleguide
- the illustrations are accurate and informative
- the book reflects the subject matter accurately and, as far as possible, completely
- the book equals or exceeds the internal standards of the writing team.

The editing task can be broken into four basic areas - initial checks, appearance/layout, technical accuracy, and the 'quality' of the words. There is usually far too much to the editing task for all of these aspects to be handled by a single person in a single pass.

10.2 Who should be the editor?

There is a tradition in publishing houses of creating an editing role and in these organisations 'the editor' is a figure of considerable authority.

Conventional editors are, however, much concerned with housestyle and are often responsible for part of the management task of getting a book from the writer to the bookshelves or magazine racks. The editors of user guides, on the other hand, have to deal much more with content and technical accuracy. Furthermore, so much has to be covered in the editing of technical documentation that it is hard to see how the idea of an omnipotent and singular managing editor could work in practical terms.

There are also a number of other considerations. In any well-ordered writing establishment - in-house or contracting - there is always a danger of a megalomaniac arising to fill what would be an unfortunate role of King Editor. This of course would be a very bad thing indeed. Further, a dedicated editor could easily lose touch with the real world of users and their needs if he was never exposed to them. If you add to this the difficulty of one person carrying out all the disparate tasks involved, a clear case develops for approaching this in a different way.

In some cases, particularly in internal writing departments, you need someone to take a higher level view of the writing as a whole and it may be appropriate to nominate this person as 'the editor'. However, theirs should be more of a supervisory role within the team, performing spot checks on different projects to ensure that quality is being maintained.

For the day-to-day editing, the problems described above must be cauterised. This can be achieved quite easily by the simple expedient of making members of the writing team edit each other's work, the writer on one job being the editor on the next and vice versa. This should solve some of the problems, although it may generate a situation where so many old scores are being settled that nothing gets done! If you adopt this approach, you must also need to bear in mind that not all writers make good editors. You must select the members of the writing team suitable for nomination to this role very carefully and according to their abilities. When you read the later sections of this chapter about the tasks to be performed in order to carry out different elements of the editing process, you will see that the temperaments required to perform the different elements may be quite different.

Just one further point on this subject. If you have a project which involves the production of a number of books, a single person must be appointed as the senior editor for the task. This person will then be responsible for ensuring that there is consistency of style and approach across all the books.

10.3 Initial checks

The first editing process should be a quick read through the book with the synopsis to hand. This should make sure that the chapters and titles established in the synopsis, and signed off by the owner, are present. If they are not, the writer must have a pretty good explanation for being rebellious. If the principles described in earlier chapters of this book have been adhered to, any change required by the writer (or owner) as a result of further investigation or a metamorphosis in ideas should have been reflected in an updated synopsis that has been signed-off by all parties.

If changes are found which cannot be explained, the book should be returned to the writer. Remember the dictionary definition at the start of this chapter and bear in mind the fact that the editor has more pips on his shoulder than the writer. In other words, the editor is king and the writer must obey.

10.4 Editing the appearance/layout

This task only becomes a consideration when a book has been desktop-published (see Figure 10.1). Whether you desktop publish before or after other aspects of the editing task have been addressed is largely a matter of personal preference. When making the decision, however, you must take the following items into consideration:

- whether the word-processed version of the book can be laid out clearly incorporating screens and other illustrations in the correct places. If the editor cannot relate the text to the planned layout quickly and easily, it will make the editing task very much more difficult. This would tend to steer you in the direction of desktop publishing prior to editing.
- whether the book includes a large number of graphic images. If edits are likely to result in the need for a large number of these images to be moved, with some desktop publishing packages this may cause a heavy overhead when entering the edits. In this case, you might opt to wait until after the edit to desktop publish.
- deadlines and balance of workloads. Obviously, there will be occasions when it might be better to desktop publish before editing, but deadlines and the relative workloads for different members of the writing team dictate otherwise.

Whenever you choose to desktop publish and whether you have one or more than one desktop publishing stages, the first person to check the appearance of a book after it has been processed through desktop publishing must be the writer. This is particularly important where another individual has prepared diagrams and desktop-published the whole document. The writer should quickly spot where errors of interpretation have occurred during this process. One example of this might be where several heading types are used - main chapter headings, section headings, paragraph headings, and so on - and the person doing the desktop publishing has misunderstood the value you want to apply to a particular title. Similarly, screens and reports may be placed in the wrong positions. Often these problems will not be noticed by the person doing the desktop publishing as he will not be familiar with the book or its contents.

If the book is subsequently to be edited through the technical and 'word quality' stages, these editors should be on the look-out for the odd error or inconsistency that has slipped through. In addition, they should be checking that the words and illustrations interact correctly, ensuring that the total message gets through.

The last stage at which the appearance and layout of the book must be checked is after all the internal edits have been incorporated and just before the book is sent out to the reviewer. This is a final check to ensure that the appearance is as specified and that no glitches have crept in at the last minute, e.g. the movement of a text item that has resulted in the desktop publishing package producing a line of ridiculously widely spaced text. If you have access to a designer, it is best to let them handle the overall appearance of the book at this stage. Their knowledge and 'eye' will always ensure that they notice errors that are invisible to mortal man.

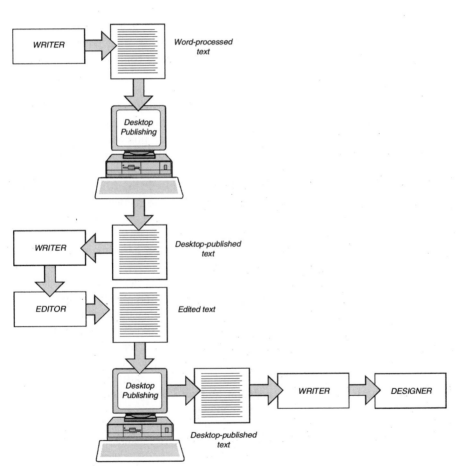

Figure 10.1
Editing desktop-published text

10.5 The technical edit

As soon as we know that the book satisfies the requirements of the synopsis in terms of content and, if necessary, it has been desktop-published and checked by the writer, the next stage is to look at it from a technical point of view.

We usually look upon the preparation of user guides as a manufacturing process rather than a branch of consultancy. If we are in the business of manufacturing, we are building products and the measure of a product's success is whether or not it works. Although books do not have working parts in the accepted sense, they must still work and achieve predetermined objectives and the technical editor is concerned with these aspects of the project. The technical editor does not have to concern him or herself with the quality of the writing. Instead he or she must ensure that the book is in the general sense complete (see Figure 10.2).

The technical edit is particularly important for user guides where a computer system is directly involved. In this case, it is essential that any screens shown are accurate and that the text does adequately describe the screens it purports to. The technical editor will, therefore, have to sit at a computer screen driving the system through according to the book.

However, the technical editor is also responsible for reading through the text and checking the sense and flow and the interaction of the text and illustration. There are, therefore, other situations where a 'technical edit' is valuable. For example, if the subject of the book is standards and procedures, the technical edit is concerned with ensuring that all the procedures make sense and flow logically from one point to the next. To give an extreme example, a fire procedure that starts by telling people to 'assemble in the car park and check in with your supervisor' and ends with telling people to 'leave by the nearest exit, always using the stairs rather than the lift' would clearly have something very wrong with its sequence.

The broad definition of a technical edit could be ensuring that the book 'works' in a mechanical sense.

If the technical editor has any queries, he may have to study source documents or even talk to end-users. The main prerequisite is that, at the outset, the technical editor has absolutely no idea about the product or service being explained other than from the pages of the book. If the technical editor cannot understand or operate the system from what he reads in the document, it is fairly likely that the user will find things difficult too.

The task of a technical editor can be an enormously difficult one. The person concerned must be extremely pedantic and nit-picking to ensure that all the relevant details have been covered. If a computer system *is* involved, the technical editor must be prepared to pick the writer up at every step if it is necessary to ensure that the poor final user is not left in a maze of bewilderment. Any of you who have been given the hapless task of trying out a piece of software on your own with minimal support will know what I am talking about!

Within moments of accessing the system, the false dawn of tiptoeing through obvious and simple options must be followed by some brave sorties into less clear and perhaps uncharted territory. In no time insolent flashing fields on the screen indicate essential information not present, and while a few attempts at putting in a date that the system seems happy to accept are usually rewarded, some fields are altogether more tricky. Sometimes the input must already be available on another file or in another part of the database, while the level of access you have been provided may well act as a universal inhibitor to any further research.

It is at times like this that the crushed writer, being human and in a hurry to meet the deadline, may have sketched out some likely looking text and with a muttered, 'Hmmm, that seems OK,' and rapid depressions of the Escape key, hightailed it back to the main menu as quickly as possible.

This of course will not do and even though the task is a difficult one, it is essential that the technical editor goes through the text in depth and ensures that nothing like this has occurred. In addition to checking that all the screens involved are described accurately and completely, the editor must ensure that no options have been missed. It has been known for the technical editor to find complete sub-menus that the writer has overlooked and blatant errors such as this are calculated to encourage deep unease in the mind of the reviewer if it were not for the attentions of the editor. Of course, this should not happen if the synopsis stage has been undertaken correctly.

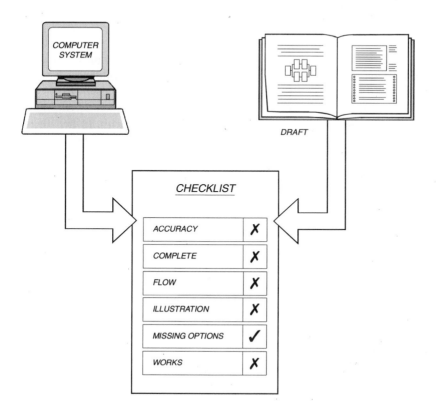

Figure 10.2
The task of the technical editor

When the technical edit has been completed, a judgement has to be made about whether to go straight on to the next editing stage, or make the amendments raised by the technical edit and reprint the document. Unless the technical changes are very light indeed, it is a very good idea to amend the document and reprint. If you try to superimpose conventional editorial changes onto a hard copy that is already well marked with technical changes, there is every chance that amendment of the document will become extremely difficult and mistakes will be made. Furthermore, technical edits tend to involve the rewriting or addition of text, so the 'word quality' editor may not be editing the words finally adopted by the writer!

So the changes should be made and the document goes onto the next editing stage.

Clearly the technical edit can be very complicated. This can be seen from the problems described above. However, if the quality of language and English style are avoided, it should be possible to concentrate on the job in hand and achieve a fair degree of success in ensuring that the book reflects the system accurately.

10.6 The 'word quality' or 'English' edit

In this, the syntax, logic, and general 'feel' of the book will be checked - by another person. We tend to call this edit a 'read', but it is really a most exhausting process. Grammar, punctuation, flow, logical thinking, and the all-important business of making sure that everything is consistent, must be one of the most tiring tasks in a writer's job specification.

How does this editor work? Well, this varies depending on the draft stage at which the edit is being undertaken, but in general the following should give some guidelines.

We will assume that, for the sake of argument, the editor is editing a full version of a book - desktop-published, paginated, and with all the diagrams, screens, and other illustrations in place. Even if editing word-processed copy, the book should be complete. Only one element may be missing at this stage: this is the index. As this is largely referenced to the page numbers, it is normal to leave the index until the final draft is signed off. It does not take much of a change to a document to 'throw' the pagination and it really is not worth tackling the index until the book is almost complete.

Front matter first. This should all be in place and the wording should be checked carefully. Remember, part of this will be couched in a legalistic way and there may be standards and precedents for this, established by the owner or the writing team.

The 'word quality' editor should first pull out the contents sheet and set this on one side. I can guarantee that there will be a discrepancy somewhere between the first draft contents sheet and the contents. It may be in the titling or the pagination, but it will be there. So, as each new chapter and section is encountered in the body of the text, the contents sheet - set aside you will remember - should be checked carefully.

Then the main body of the book. The editor must read each and every word in the document. Obviously, he or she must check all the aspects described at the start of this section. As we said at the outset, this book is not about explaining grammatical construction and the correct use of the English language. The person nominated for this task should have a good and clear understanding of what is required. However, this editor also needs to act as a proof-reader and in the next few paragraphs we outline some particular items to look out for (see Figure 10.3).

Spelling. As we said earlier, the spell-checker will not pick up errors that are, in fact, valid words, e.g. on for won, there for their, wring for writing, fore and four and for, files for flies, all get through. It is also easy to misread these, but the one thing you can be sure of is that, if one of these appears in the first few pages, the reviewer will spot it and immediately berate the writer for carelessness. In addition words may have been added to a spell-checker dictionary in error. The spell-checker may then actually overlook wrong spellings, which is distinctly unnerving!

The editor should also remember that the spell-checker may accept culturally unacceptable spellings. My spell-checker accepts organize - because that is what it came with - and organise - because I added it to the dictionary. I may, therefore, introduce inconsistency into my text which the spell-checker will overlook. The editor needs to know the standards for these words and ensure they are adhered to.

That old carrot of the the repetition is another one to trip up the editor. It will not be spotted by all spell-checkers - but again you can bet some eagle-eyed end user will will notice this sort of of error.

Some words and contractions look extremely odd on the printed page. Consider ie, for that is, or eg to represent for example. The way I have used them here happens too quickly for the reader and the best way of slowing down the process and ensuring that the reader has 'got your drift' is to use the old full punctuation method of 'i.e.' as in 'your full address, i.e. your name, number, street, town, post-town (if one), county, and postcode'. Problems to watch out for are the above, plus Id (as in User Id), function keys which if not 'lifted' by a graphic symbol need to be stressed. This could be done by the use of brackets [F9], [PF12], [Enter], [PgDn], etc., italicising, emboldening, change of font, or any other appropriate technique. The editor should also look out for the use of etc., and anything else that is very small or misleading.

As is discussed elsewhere, the editor should look very hard indeed for inconsistencies of style. Changes of tense and voice, subtle moves from one mood to another - all will confuse the reader and make for a jerky, clumsy book. Although editors tend to notice these things far more than most readers, they should not compromise themselves, but liberally use the red pen when in

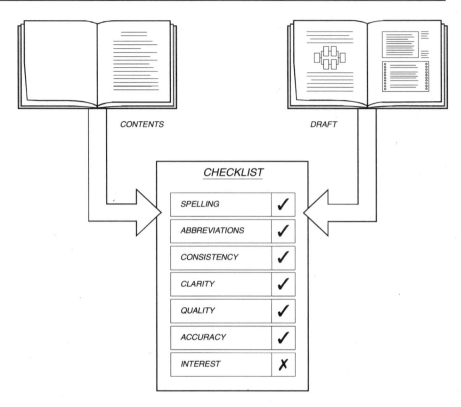

Figure 10.3
The task of the
word quality editor

any doubt. The editor should also watch out for flights of fancy. A user guide is not an appropriate place for a writer to emulate the likes of Tolstoy or Shakespeare. User guides are working books.

10.7 Who should make the corrections?

It is not the editor's job to make the corrections on the electronic file - that is the work of the writer. Although in a well-ordered writing establishment, no one should 'own' a book after the first draft has been written, Chinese whispers set in with a vengeance if Mr A writes it, Misses B, C, and D edit and correct it and send it off to the reviewer.

When he has read the book, who does the reviewer complain to? Mr A no longer recognises his work and the editors worked in different ways on different aspects of the editing process. In addition, Mr A may have intelligence about the reasons for writing things in particular ways that the editors may not be party to. Much better, all in all, for the original writer to incorporate the changes - at least at first draft stage. After that, anyone can field the second and final draft edits, which should be small.

10.8 Editor's marks

While I am the world's worst at using the recognised system of editor's marks, there is a great deal to be said for keeping to the rules. A full set of marks can be found in books describing print production. A sub-set of those you will probably find most useful is provided below.

INSTRUCTION	TEXTUAL MARK	MARGINAL MARK
Leave unchanged	technical authors	(STET)
Insert new matter	technical/authors	followed by new matter
Delete and leave a space	technical/authors	
Delete and close up	technical/authors	
Substitute character or part of one or more words	technical authors	
Insert full stop or decimal point, colon, semicolon, or comma	technical authors	or or or
Insert apostrophe or quotation marks	technical authors	
Insert hyphen	technical/authors	
Start new paragraph	Technical authors	or (np)
No fresh paragraph, run on	technical authors. The advice	or (ro)
Transpose characters or words	authors technical	or (Trs.)
Transpose lines	professional skill technical author's	or (Trs.)

INSTRUCTION	TEXTUAL MARK	MARGINAL MARK
Centre	[technical authors]	[ ]
Indent	technical authors	⊏
Cancel indent	←technical authors	⊐
Move matter to the right	[technical authors]→	⊏
Move matter to the left	←[technical authors]	⊐
Take characters, words, or line to next line, column, or page	technical authors	⊏
Take characters, words, or line back to the previous line, column, or page	technical authors]	⊐
Delete space between characters or words	technical author s	◠
Insert space between characters or words	technical authors	Y
Reduce space between characters or words	technical authors	⋔
Insert space between lines or paragraphs	technical authors professional skill	—<
Reduce space between lines or paragraphs	technical authors professional skill	—)
Set in or change to italic	technical authors	⊔
Set in or change to capital letters	technical authors	≡

10.9 Summary

When all the editing is done, the writer should feel fairly confident about his or her book. If the book is going in to the reviewer as a first draft, it will conform to the style agreed in the synopsis. It will have been investigated conscientiously and written carefully. It will then have been checked by editors at two levels - and at each level the writer will have read the comments of the editors and made appropriate changes to the text (see Figure 10.4). He should also have learned from the process as writing is a skill that you will never totally master.

So the combined efforts of writer, designer, and two editors ride along with the first draft. Second and subsequent drafts are meant to be refinements of the first draft, so the editing process should be a great deal more straightforward, but the principles described above should still be followed in full if any new material is added to the book. Editing should not be seen as a chore - it is the 'vitally necessary evil' - and it, more than any other activity, will ensure that your book is second to none.

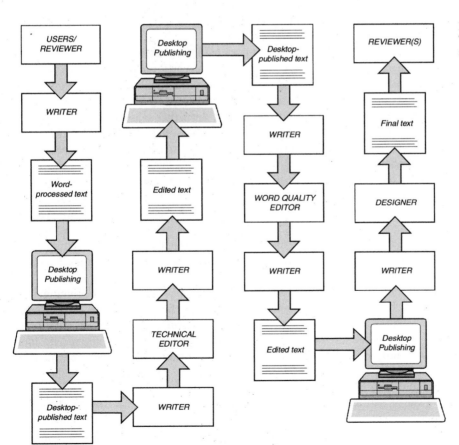

Figure 10.4
The ideal editing sequence

11 Maintaining the confidence of the owner

The ultimate object of any documentation exercise is to produce documents that the users will read, find useful, and that can make the owner feel proud. Earlier chapters in this book have described the process that the writing team must follow in order to ensure that they produce books of the highest quality. There are, however, many stages along the way. A wrong step at any stage may severely dent the confidence that the reviewer, and thus the owner, has in the writer.

Many of the processes described up until now are entirely invisible to the reviewer. Some of the processes he will see early on in the project may not be entirely encouraging. For example the writer will be asking all sorts of questions that, to the reviewer, may have ridiculously obvious answers and for a long spell prior to first draft production, the writer may disappear altogether!

So, how does the writer ensure that the reviewer and the owner do not lose faith? Well, aside from ensuring that he keeps the quality right and adheres to any standards and timescales that have been set, the main answer to this is by keeping the reviewer informed about what is happening. It is very important that the reviewer understands what the project stages are, what he should expect to happen at each stage, and what he is required to do. This is particularly important where the reviewer is acting as a co-ordinator, passing drafts out for other people to read. In this instance he will be setting those people's expectations and will be first one in the firing line if they have any complaints.

If it can be arranged, holding a kick-off meeting at the beginning of a project, bringing together everyone who will be involved at the different investigation and review stages, can set things off to a good start. The writer can then explain in some detail what will be happening and try to win their hearts and minds. Unfortunately, this is often not possible, because of geographical reasons or because the numbers of people involved make it too difficult. It is always worth considering though.

Even if a full kick-off meeting is not possible, the writer should always sit down with the reviewer at the start of the project to explain the various stages and what he will need from the reviewer at each stage. Whilst it is relatively easy to explain that you want to interview people and identify who you want to see and when, explaining what should be going on at the different review stages is rather more complex. There need to be very specific instructions about what should be expected at each stage and what people are required to do.

11.1   Preliminary discussions

The writer's early discussions with the reviewer need to explain that technical writing is very much a collaborative process, combining the skills of the writing team with the knowledge, inventiveness, and requirements of the owner of the book. Consequently, the quality of the finished product is heavily dependent on the practical support provided by the reviewer, users, and development team during the documentation project. Furthermore, in order that the reviewer can ensure that the writing team is progressing along the right lines, there are a number of stages in the documentation process when the writer gives him or her the opportunity to adopt the role of schoolteacher and 'mark the work'.

The writer should then outline the stages to be adopted in his particular project. Generally speaking, these stages will be:

1.   The synopsis and design styleguide
2.   The first draft
3.   The second draft
4.   The final draft
5.   The preparation of the index.

This should be followed by a description of the reviewer's role in the project, explaining that his main role is to co-ordinate the project and manage the review process and he must ensure he is given sufficient authority to do this.

The writer must go on to explain that he wants the reviewer and his nominated representatives to read what has been written and look at what has been designed. This having been done, it is necessary for the writer to be told about the shortcomings, errors, and omissions, so that the document can be corrected and the project can progress to the next stage. It should be clear that the ultimate objective is to produce a document of which all those involved can be proud, and which can be published and sent out to users and customers.

11.2   Sign-off documents

It is one thing to shuffle up to the reviewer of a book and obtain a surly, ' ... looks OK', between bites of a cheese and pickle French stick and telephone calls to his broker (or was it his bookmaker?) and quite another to get a sign-off on a pre-prepared form. If the reviewer has to sign documents off at each stage in their life cycle, he will take very considerable care over the process. So the writer will be well advised to insist that at each of the major stages in the project the reviewer formally signs to agree that progress to that stage has met his expectations.

By definition, work should not commence on a project stage until a sign-off has been obtained for the previous stage. It is essential to obtain specific agreement at every step as a prerequisite to a successful project. To start writing before agreement is obtained, or worse, where agreement is never obtained, is to invite disaster and give the wrong impression to the reviewer. Collaboration shares out responsibility and authority in equal measure between the writer and the reviewer.

11.3   General pointers for reviewers

Once the project rules have been established, the writer must go on to explain the general principles to be adopted when reviewing documents. The most obvious ones are to ensure that all the people most concerned with the project examine the documents to be reviewed, and that if several people are involved in a review, the principal reviewer must collate all their comments onto one document. This latter policy allows any internal conflicts to be resolved before the document returns to the writer.

In addition, the reviewer should be advised to use a red pen to mark comments on the document. This sounds trivial, but you would be amazed at how much more a mark in red ink leaps out from a black and white page than one in black or blue. If the writer misses a review comment, it is bound to be picked up and this is something that can cause the writer to lose face and the reviewer confidence.

The reviewer also needs to be reminded that the writer is not a mind reader, and the draft must not be returned with comments like 'rubbish' or 'more information required'. The writer must be told exactly what is wrong with the document, and the reviewer must ensure that amendments or additions to be inserted are to be written out in full, comments are marked clearly, and they are unequivocal. Brief notes may be clear to those in the know, but 'clear as mud' to the writer.

Another suggestion to be made, albeit an obvious one, is that, if the draft is to be sent through the post or an internal mail system, the document with the review comments on it should be photocopied before it is returned to the writer. A reviewer who has spent hours poring over a hot copy of a book, marking it up clearly and precisely, will not feel happy if he loses his only copy to the vagaries of the postal system.

Finally, it is worth pointing out that reviewers will make better progress if they are on their own without interruptions. So it is advisable to obtain the use of an office or other quiet area when editing.

11.4 The synopsis and design styleguide

This is the first document people will be called on to review. In addition to the reviewer, any senior personnel involved with the project should read and comment on it. They must remember that the synopsis is a very important document which sets out very clearly what the final books will contain.

The reviewer and any other readers of the synopsis and styleguide must be made aware that the synopsis is essentially an outline of the book to be produced, telling the reader what writing style will be adopted, the purpose of the book, and the audience at which it is targeted. They must know that it should outline the contents of the book, specify the book and chapter titles, provide a brief description of the contents of each chapter, and include a list of each of the menu options, screens, or procedures to be described.

Those looking at the design styleguide should expect it to incorporate any features laid down by the owner or requested by the reviewer, that it should consist of several pages of some text presented in the style to be adopted for the finished documentation, and that it will show the page size and layout to be adopted, the typefaces to be used, the header and footer styles, examples of most of the ways in which text will be presented, and diagram styling.

Turnaround in two weeks is a good target to set for the reviewer of the synopsis. If, as a result of the review process, it is necessary to make amendments and resubmit the synopsis and styleguide, the reviewer should aim to check the revisions and return his comments within two days. It must always be clear that work on the next stage will not start until the synopsis and styleguide have been signed off.

11.4.1 Points to check

The reviewer of the synopsis should be encouraged to:

- look carefully at the overall structure and content of the proposed document to ensure that it contains the information he expects and the sequence of information presented is acceptable.
- check the detailed contents to ensure that every option, screen, or procedure is covered somewhere, and that all the major points to be covered in the final document are mentioned somewhere in the synopsis.
- check the writing style to ensure it is acceptable.
- ensure the book is aimed at the right audience. The reviewer must try to put himself in the position of a typical reader and ask the following questions: Is it pitched at the right level? Is the structure in line with the needs of the audience? Will the use of this book result in a real understanding of the product, service, or procedure?
- ensure the style and typeface conform to any corporate standards adopted by the owner organisation.

- check that he is happy with the proposed size, typeface, header and footer styling, and page numbering.
- consider whether he is happy with the overall 'look and feel' of the document.
- consider whether the document will 'work' properly. In other words, if maintenance of the book is a factor, have the appropriate methods - loose-leaf binders, maintainable pagination systems, etc. - been proposed?

It is vital that this document is reviewed carefully. Once it has been signed off it will form the basis for the first draft. If the writing style is changed, or new system options are added, or the appearance is changed, after this stage there may be an increased cost and delay in the project. The reviewer must be made very aware of this.

11.5 The first draft

This is the first copy of the actual book that the reviewer will see. It is what, based on the investigations and the synopsis, the writer thinks is required. In addition to the reviewer, it should be read by personnel with an in-depth knowledge of the product, service, or procedures that are the subject of the book and also by senior personnel involved with the project.

It is important that the reviewer is made aware of what he should expect at this stage. That is the first draft should be more than 80 per cent correct. This often does not mean very much to people. However, if the reviewer is made aware that even with 80 per cent correct there is quite a considerable amount of room for amendments - out of every 100 pages, the equivalent of approximately 20 pages might need complete change, he will have an appreciation both of what he should anticipate seeing, and the size of the task ahead of him. Obviously this level of edit represents a great deal of red ink and the reviewer will need to be reassured that this is quite acceptable - the writer is not going to be either offended or defensive about this. The objective of both parties is, after all, a book that is as near perfect as can be achieved.

This is the most important review stage of all. It is at this stage that the writer must ask the reviewer to make a major effort to ensure that any errors that may have been made are identified, explained, and rectified. The reviewer must make sure that nothing is left unconsidered, in the knowledge that it can be addressed at second draft stage. He must be aware that the second draft stage is not another opportunity to undertake a major review of the book, but simply an opportunity to check that the amendments marked up at first draft have been incorporated. The reviewer should consider the first draft to be the one opportunity to correct errors and omissions, and that the adoption of this approach makes it possible to progress very swiftly from first to final draft.

This review is of course substantial. It is not always easy for the reviewer and any other readers involved to set aside the time required for the review. It is essential, however, that it is done correctly and that it takes place within a reasonable timescale. Three weeks is a good target completion date at this stage. It is up to the reviewer to ensure that all the readers complete their tasks satisfactorily in this time frame. Due to other commitments, this stage can stretch out enormously if allowed to do so. I am aware of at least one project where the first draft reviews took between six months and a year! Sometimes the reviewer can be encouraged to get things moving by a gentle reminder that work on the second draft will not begin until the first draft is signed off and all review comments have been received, and that delays at this stage will impact severely on the project.

11.5.1 *Points to check*

The reviewer of the first draft should be encouraged to check that:

- the text is accurate and the products, services, or procedures have been portrayed accurately
- no essential detail has been left out
- the draft matches the synopsis and styleguide
- the terminology particular to the products, services, procedures, and company has been used correctly
- a consensus has been reached for internal disputes about correct explanations
- no points have been left for resolution in a future draft - all substantial changes must be included at this stage
- any screen layouts and reports that have been included are valid and representative, not commercially sensitive. And, if necessary, replacements have been provided.

It is vital that this document is reviewed carefully. Once it has been signed off it will form the basis for the second draft. There will be no further opportunity to amend the text, other than for typographical errors or errors arising from misunderstanding of the first draft comments. The reviewer must be made very aware of this.

It is vital that this document is reviewed carefully. Once signed off, it forms the basis for the production of the second draft.

11.6 The second draft

This is the second copy of the book that the reviewer will see. It is produced by incorporating their comments from the first draft review process. The reviewer should expect the second draft to be more than 95 per cent correct.

This book must be read by someone considered competent enough to check that the first draft edits have been adequately incorporated into the second draft. They should remember that they do not have to check any text that was unchanged in the first draft.

This should be a fairly easy review, since only edits are being checked, not the technical accuracy of the book as a whole. Turnaround in two weeks is a suitable target to set at this stage. It must be made clear to the reviewer that work on the final draft will not begin until the second draft is signed off and all review comments have been received.

11.6.2 Points to check

The reviewer of the second draft must check that all amendments made to the first draft have been incorporated.

The reviewer should be made aware that once signed off, the second draft forms the basis for the production of the final draft. The only changes after this should be for typographical errors.

11.7 The final draft

This is the final copy of the book. It is produced by incorporating the comments from the second draft review process. The reviewer should expect the final draft to be 100 per cent correct. This review may be carried out by anyone considered competent enough to check that the second draft edits have been adequately incorporated into the final draft.

As with the second draft review, this task should be fairly simple and the review should be completed within two weeks. The reviewer should be made aware that work on the index will not begin until the final draft is signed off.

11.8 The index

This is the last item that the reviewer will be called upon to check. The index should only be prepared once the final draft has been signed off and the writer is sure that the pagination will not change. The index should provide a clear and easy way for the readers to access information in the book.

The index should be checked by senior personnel involved with the project. At this stage production is only waiting for this final sign-off, so the reviewer should be encouraged to complete the review as soon as possible. A turn-around of about one week is an appropriate target to set.

If, as a result of the review, changes are required, the writer should make the changes and resubmit the index. The review of the revisions should take place within two days of their submission.

11.8.1 Points to check

The reviewer must check that:

- all important topics appear in the index
- all page references are correct
- the index is easy to follow.

11.9 Conclusion

As you can see, the role of a document reviewer is quite demanding. However, it is vitally important and worthwhile as it keeps the owner involved in the process of documentation and at the same time ensures that the writer is providing exactly what the owner requires.

12 Management of the documentation process

From what you have been reading, it will be apparent that writing user guides takes place on a totally different planet from the preparation of text for a novel. The writing of user guides is a manufacturing process, pure and simple. It may be creative; it may also require the employment of knowledge, experience, and understanding. But so does any other manufacturing process especially where products are, like user guides, being made to order.

I used to fancy myself as being a form of consultant, bringing learned wisdom into the field of play, but I now have a simpler view of things. There is no difference between what I do and what a bridge builder or a plumber does. Faced with a simply expressed requirement - bridge this estuary, supply books to describe 'X' - I have to gauge the extent of a job and calculate the need for human and other resources. The costs and benefits have to be presented to the eventual owner in the form of a proposal. In the event of the project being agreed, I have to apply the resources and measure the time taken against the plan. In order that the owner can see that progress is being made, I have developed stages throughout the manufacturing process that show what has been achieved. Finally, as my company acts as a contractor, I have to collect fees at predetermined stages and hopefully make a profit.

That all sounds like making things to me!

And the role and operation of a writing company is much like a company's internal writing department or even the lone technical author - self-employed or staff member. All must be effective and make a useful contribution - in short, be 'profitable'.

Like any manufacturing process, constraints and responsibilities are applied to writer, reviewer, and owner (these are described in some detail elsewhere in this book). The suggestion of constraints and responsibilities implies a need for management and, whilst each of the stages in the documentation process has been discussed in detail in the preceding chapters, we will use this chapter to stress some of the specific points to watch while managing a writing project.

One of the main dangers in a writing project is that the task is, quite literally, 'shelved' - usually at a late stage in the process. A surprising number of software implementations are never completed, and this almost inevitably means that the documentation is initially set aside and then unceremoniously 'dumped'.

This situation obviously has cost implications. Furthermore, there is little satisfaction to be gained from working on a project that is not completed. Like a shipyard, we all want to see the launch even though it heralds the beginning of the end for the project. You should always remember that a very considerable amount of time will be spent on the work before a single word is set down, if you follow the advice in this book. If willingness to complete a writing project seems to flag, the owner will have to be convinced that a book that is shelved when three-quarters written, will perhaps have reached 95 per cent of the required levels of effort and borne 95 per cent of the cost.

At the end of the process, providing the job *is* completed, with books sitting on shelves or being happily thumbed by confident users throughout an organisation, the manager of the writing project might do well to reflect on the nature of the task just ended. He will have to admit that his management job was as much about people as it was about books. And, what a diverse collection of people were involved in the work! The writers and editors of course, and any designer, illustrator, or desktop publishing operator he was fortunate enough to employ, but also the people from the owning organisation - the reviewer or reviewers - and the users - not only from the point of view of trying to satisfy their needs but also when they acted as sources of valuable information.

Management of the writing process is about three main things - setting out the stages and methods carefully, ensuring that things happen as they should, and behaving with courage and fortitude to the ultimate success of the project, even when things go horribly wrong.

12.1 Defining the production stages

There have been many indications in the previous chapters of the processes that should be adopted in the development of documentation. Not all will be appropriate to all projects, but, by and large, it is all there. A simplified diagram of the stages (Figure 12.1) may help to put this all into context.

If you accept the analogy of the technical writing exercise as a manufacturing process, each stage must be controlled as in a factory. As in many conventional batch-based production processes, some of the major stages may be split down into a series of smaller processes. There are three principle stages in the documentation stages where this occurs: preparation of the first draft, preparation of the second draft, and preparation of the final draft.

Figure 12.1
The documentation
stages

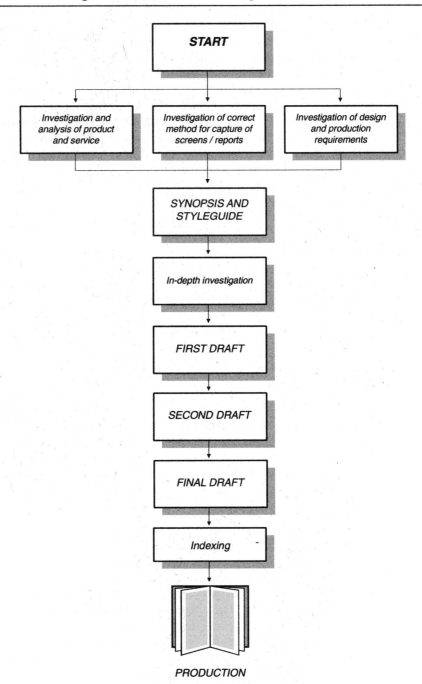

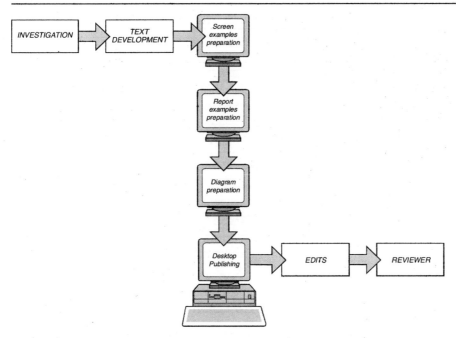

Figure 12.2
The first draft
preparation process

The first draft process is the most complex for the writer, since so many different elements are involved (Figure 12.2). The second draft edit, whilst relatively straightforward for the writer, is complicated by the input of the reviewer (Figure 12.3) (shopkeeping would be so easy without customers!).

Even the final draft, although involving very minor changes, must go through a number of processes to ensure that quality is not lost through carelessness at the last hurdle (Figure 12.4).

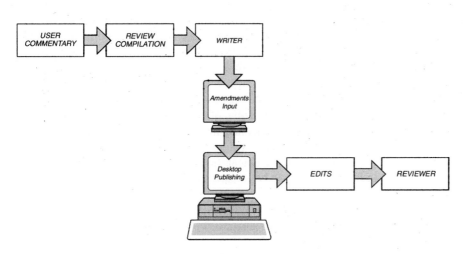

Figure 12.3
Second draft
preparation

Figure 12.4
Final draft preparation

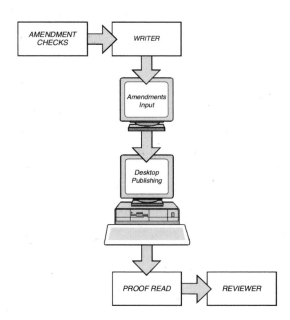

Furthermore, each of the first and second draft stages includes an editing element. This is composed of a number of processes as shown in Figure 12.5.

12.2 Setting a schedule

If it is possible to set out the production stages, it is also possible to identify the work centres in which each must be carried out, and apply people and dates to each stage. This can become fairly complex and the computer-competent readers of this book will think in terms of computerising the process. This, too, is entirely possible, but a big chart on the wall will suffice. Even with upwards of seventy books 'in the mill' at one time, *we* use a chart and find that this provides graphic and accurate detail from which to make scheduling decisions.

Allocating work to a strict schedule and to individuals is a notoriously difficult process, often exacerbated by the low priority given to the documentation task. Most users and reviewers, if also responsible for other tasks that may result in the generation of revenue, will give precedence to those tasks. This can result in cancelled meetings and resultant delays in the project. If a schedule has been defined, the incidence of this can be considerably reduced. The management in all areas will be able to see the delay and, therefore, potential additional cost incurred as a result of changes in schedule. The schedule will also keep the writers on their toes - discouraging them from indulging in flights of fantasy and imagination (to which, unfortunately, we are all far too prone) and concentrating their minds on the job in hand.

Figure 12.5
The editing processes

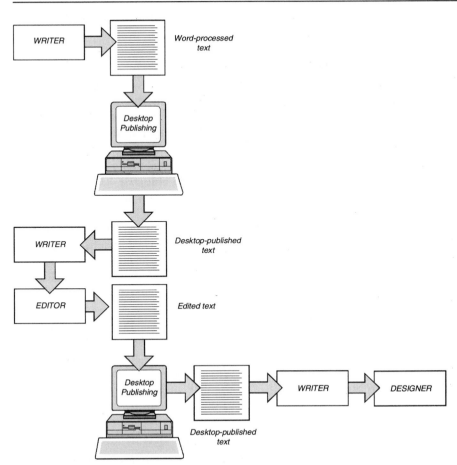

Writers are a rather fussy lot who derive most pleasure in their jobs from doing their work well. They can have a great deal to contend with and are, by and large, maids of all work and masters of many. They usually dislike starting a job when critical aspects of the task are either incomplete or simply not available at all. Unfortunately, the nature of the job almost determines an incomplete portfolio - some of the menu options will not work, part of the system will not have been specified, some of the screen images are not on the diskette that comes through the post, those screens that have appeared contain meaningless gibberish - and the writer often has to work around the problem, trying to complete the information himself instead of bleating loud and long about the dried-up supply.

This can have a negative effect on throughput and also reduces the quality of life so valued by the writer. Again, much of this can be avoided with careful scheduling and definition of responsibilities at the start of the project. If the essential elements and responsibilities are all defined in the schedule, it is then up to the managers in all areas affected to ensure that the milestones set on the schedule are met.

There is, of course, a basic problem of scheduling each writing task. Writing, thank goodness, is not often made the subject of a time-and-motion study exercise, and it is very difficult to say that such and such a job will go into the first cut of the text at 10.30 a.m. on the 6th and be out at 4.30 p.m. on the 30th. Elsewhere in this book you will find very rough figures for the expected output from a writer but, of course, these will vary according to their responsibilities. A writer who is also an editor will be dividing his or her time between these tasks. A writer on a project where details for screens and reports have to be manually keyed in rather than given to him on a disk, will probably have his productivity reduced as a result. As with any task, only experience will really show how much time needs to be allocated in any given situation.

Some writers must be watched like hawks. It is one thing to know how much the writer *should* be writing for a project and schedule time accordingly, and quite another to know how much they *will* write about a given subject. If the consensus is that a piece of work will take 2,000 words to describe properly, and the writer goes off on a whim and takes 5,000, naturally the allocated time is unlikely to be sufficient.

Similarly, if the source information is not available and the writer is allowed to go off on a detective's trail rather than placing the onus on those truly responsible, schedules can be affected. The writer may emerge triumphant like a latter-day Philip Marlowe, with all that is required, but not a word written in a period of several hours.

12.3 Soothing the battered ego

The other aspect that has to be handled carefully is the bruised ego. Writers quickly learn the foibles of others in their team - a tendency to end sentences with the word 'it', a nasty habit of using the words 'get' and 'got', being forgetful about using the spell-checker coupled with a form of insanity that results in the word 'the' frequently being spelled 'teh'. Now, while they may learn to know and love these quirky human errors when editing the work of another, they may have difficulties when this person carries out an edit on their work. Even if you have a dedicated editor, the writer may feel hurt at the amount of criticism that his 'baby' has incurred. The prospects for the writer taking offence and becoming very defensive after the first review are even greater.

This has to be stamped on hard. It is important that every writer understands and appreciates that the editorial process is all part of raising the quality and their ultimate satisfaction in their work. The editor or reviewer should not be seen as the gorgon-in-waiting, ready to turn the writer to stone with one withering look. Everyone makes mistakes, but even those with undoubted flaws in their writing style can be good writers and, indeed, make very good editors.

Constructive criticism and its absorption by the writer are essential to the success of a writing project, the eventual contentment of the readers of the books, and the fulfilment felt by the writer.

12.4 Working with designers, illustrators, and desktop publishing operators

Design, illustration, and desktop publishing could of course all be performed by the writer - in which case most of the difficulties described below will not arise. If, however, you are involving specialists in areas other than writing, you must be aware of the pitfalls.

A key thing to remember with people in all three of these areas is just what they are there for. Their tasks are all part of the preparation of a book that is visually appealing and arresting. It is not their job to understand the detail of what the writer learns - on the whole, they just do not have the time.

If they are not there to learn the intricacies of a computer system from the words of the writer, clearly the original ideas for diagrams and illustrations must come from the writer. This requires the writer to sketch out some ideas and present them to the designer or illustrator - every time, and not say to the person concerned, 'do you think you could read this piece of work and give me one or two ideas?'

A major issue here is one of ignorance on the part of the writer as to what his ideas will actually mean to the other people. Even in this book written and edited by supposedly experienced writers, some of the outline sketches prepared for diagrams resulted in almost terminal hysteria from our long-suffering designer. Many of our ideas were either too large or too complicated to work and, while a picture is worth a thousand words, there are limitations to what even the best illustrator can achieve.

Experienced illustrators have an annoying habit of knowing just how much of an idea can be conveyed to the reader in a single diagram. Just as the writer will develop skills that overcome perception limitations on the part of the reader by describing ideas slowly, so the illustrator knows that it is just not possible to explain an entire computer system in a quick diagram. Consequently, when a writer knocks a very complex diagram together in a rough for the illustrator to prepare, there is a chance that it will be rejected on the grounds of being too complex. It *is* possible to show a complete production control system on a single diagram, but do *not* ask an illustrator to fit it into an A5 page layout - and do not ask a reader to comprehend it either.

Even if the writer is only obtaining help in the desktop publishing area, he must not make any assumptions. If the person who wrote the book is not doing the desktop publishing, the copy that he passes across to the person performing this role must be clearly marked to show the different elements (heading levels, positioning of illustrations, chapter and section numbers, etc.) - the desktop publishing operator is no more a mind reader than the writer is and must be given clear guidance.

12.5 Co-ordination and liaison with owners and their representatives

If they are new to the business of producing user documentation, the company for whom the writing is being generated is unlikely to appreciate just how much work is involved in the development of text, so such things as cost, the time it all takes to do, and the occupation of their offices or the time of their staff may all be cause for considerable irritation.

Furthermore, as I said earlier, problems can arise when the appointed representatives of the owner perceive other tasks as having greater commercial benefit. Some of them may just find the idea of involvement in the writing task uninteresting or frightening, and avoid making their contribution for as long as possible.

Scheduling, making them understand their responsibilities (and the limitation of their responsibilities), and strong project management on the behalf of the reviewer, can all serve to alleviate these problems. It may help to prepare a short booklet for the reviewer explaining how you are proposing to work and how you will need to interface with the owner's representatives. These factors are described in some detail in Chapter 11. He may not read your booklet, or having read it may not pass the information on to others, but at least you have tried and they should at least have an impression of the number of stages you will have to go through to 'get the manuals out'.

When the investigations involve talking to real users, there is sometimes a danger that they begin to look upon a writer as a sort of social worker. What starts out as a simple discussion about a business procedure can turn into a long and sometimes tearful diatribe about workloads, working hours, draughts around the doors, poor lighting, and bullying husbands. Furthermore, all sorts of departmental rivalries can come to light during an investigation - particularly difficult if it is between the users and system developers.

This puts the writer into a difficult position, as he must be seen as the friend to the user, or the information he needs will not be forthcoming. On the other hand, there is a job to do, and too much time spent sorting out the incidental will divert effort and time from the task in hand. The best way to handle the drift away from the subject is to be sympathetic and agree to think about the problem. Sometimes it is politic to mention things to one of the owner's senior personnel while other times diplomacy dictates a deeper discretion. These little wanderings from the point can, of course, be very valuable to the writer as they may pinpoint areas of concern that the books must address.

The books must achieve something concrete. If they do not they are an indulgence. User guides must work and that means they must do something worthwhile in the workplace. Those users with their human frailties, their skills, their knowledge, and their wisdom are the final judges of the work we do and our justification for calling ourselves writers of user documentation. To satisfy them and get the users' seal of approval, we must appear sympathetic to their needs and address those that we can through the documentation we produce. As ever, the writer will have to temper his sympathy for the user and the time spent in listening to their woes with the need to meet a schedule.

12.6 Change of reviewer

Sometimes, often through circumstances beyond their control, owners find it necessary to substitute their most important contribution to the project - the reviewer. The person with whom the writer has built a deep and mutually respectful business relationship, and who seemed to be in with the bricks, is suddenly transferred to the owner's Sarawak office. Of course his replacement may be sweetness and light, respecting the work and thinking that has gone into the project so far, and going along with decisions that have been made - even if not entirely in agreement. On the other hand, the writer may be landed with someone who makes Goebbels look like one of the most sensitive of the Samaritans. His ideas are different, he wants to make his mark, and he sees the writer as a soft footfall on his ladder to success.

In this situation gentle reasoning is always a good starting point. If necessary, however, a more senior owner representative may have to be called in to arbitrate and decide whether the project is to continue along the previously signed-off lines or whether the owner is prepared to bear the cost of making the changes newly introduced.

12.7 Conclusion

Having read this, you see that there are a variety of ways in which a project may run into trouble, missing scheduled deadlines and conflict arising out of dissent being not the least of them. It is possible, however, with a strong hand on the rein to have satisfied readers and a contented writing team.

13 Some basic lessons in document production - getting books onto shelves

Part of the initial investigation will include questions about the form in which the finished product will appear when paper-based books are required. This will include discussions about paper size and the fonts favoured by the owner, but it will also need to embrace questions about the final production method to be adopted. This encompasses details such as whether or not the book(s) will be printed or simply photocopied, the type of binding required, and any special requirements generated by virtue of the environment in which the books are to be used. In addition, there will be considerations such as budgets, image, available facilities, the quantities of books required, and how often the books will change.

So what must the writer bear in mind when making recommendations about production? Indeed, should the writer make recommendations at all, or should this be a matter entirely for those responsible for print production in the owner organisation? There is an argument that says recommendations of this sort put the writer into a no-win situation. Whatever he or she suggests will ultimately be proved wrong. However, to an extent, the final production method will have some bearing on the books' accessibility to the user family, and the writer must make sure that the work meets the requirements of the audience - and that includes the presentation method adopted.

13.1 The alternatives

In order to make recommendations, the writer must first understand the various alternatives available. These, broadly speaking, fall into the following categories:

- the printing method
- the type of binding to be adopted
- the materials to be used.

13.1.1 The printing method

The first decision here will be whether to print or photocopy. Each has its own advantages and they should be considered on their relative merits.

If you decide to print your books, there are two methods of production that you should consider. It is assumed in this day and age that typesetting user guides is a thing of the past. The normal (and more cost-effective) approach is to take the output from a desktop publishing package and submit it to a printer. The type of output required will depend on the production method you choose, but both methods ultimately result in the printer using camera-ready artwork to prepare 'plates' (paper for short runs and metal for longer runs) for use in the printing process. The alternatives are shown in Figure 13.1.

In the first method, providing a lower quality end result, you produce the camera-ready artwork from the laser printer in your own offices. The printer uses this as the basis for the creation of the plates. In the second method you supply your desktop publishing files directly to the printer. He then subjects them to an electronic image setting process, the camera-ready output from which is used to create the plates.

The electronic image setting process is really very good indeed. The camera-ready output it produces is sharp and precise, and it takes a trained eye to really appreciate the difference between print produced in this way and that which has been typeset. Print generated from plates created from laser-printed artwork will still be good, but, since the quality of the original artwork is lower, this will be reflected in the final result.

Photocopying is essentially a cheap and cheerful solution. Explanation of the process is I think unnecessary. However, you should remember that some of the professional high-quality photocopying services can produce far better results than those you may see from your ancient battered machine in the corner. Indeed, with the current state of photocopier technology, it can be very difficult to see the difference between a high-quality photocopy and print generated from laser-printed camera-ready artwork.

13.1.2 The type of binding required

A number of options are available in this area. In summary, your book may be:

- loose-leaf ring bound
- perfect bound
- stitched or stapled
- wiro bound
- comb bound.

The loose-leaf ring binder is, I am sure, the option first thought of by those with experience of computer systems and really requires no further explanation. Binders are available in a variety of sizes and qualities to meet various needs.

Figure 13.1
The production
methods

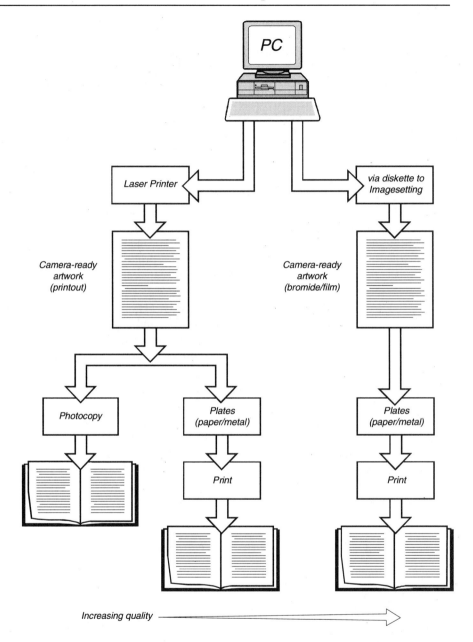

There are, of course, some size constraints. At the lower end, a document comprising ten to fifteen pages may look rather foolish in a binder. On the other hand, if you try to put too large a book in a ring binder it will always be unwieldy - but since you are going to take my advice about book length this won't be a problem for you!

Perfect binding is the method used for the production of this book. Essentially all the pages are held together by glue applied to the spine of the book. This is a good solution for documents between 48 and 200 pages long. You will find that for books shorter than this it may be difficult to open the pages of the books fully, and for longer books the additional weight will tend to put pressure on the spine, often leading to it breaking.

Stitching or stapling is a good binding method for small documents up to 48 pages in length. This is the method of binding used for most magazines, and is particularly good for small booklets that can look slightly ridiculous bound in any other way. Naturally, a stitched book cannot be maintained.

Wiro binding is not a method I would like to encourage because it can look so unattractive. However, it has some benefits and so deserves a mention. This is a method whereby the pages are held together by a wire passing through a series of holes drilled into the pages of the book. This method will probably be familiar to you from the reporters notepads, and other similar notebooks, available from most stationers. Wiro's main merit is that it is cheap (always guaranteed to bring a smile to your boss's face!).

Comb binding I really would not recommend. Like wiro it is a cheap option, and it works in a similar way. However, unlike wiro, it is usually made of a flexible plastic which does not provide a firm grip on the pages. Although this does not matter so much for a report that has a relatively short life span, it can be more of a problem with a user guide - if the spine disintegrates and all the pages flutter gently in a random order to the floor, you will have a very unhappy user!

13.1.3 The materials to be used

This section could be very short or very long, so I have opted for the former. Suffice it to say that a wide range of papers are available for the body of your document. The quality and weight of the paper will affect the cost, so you will need to exercise some discretion in this area. When choosing paper, you will need to remember that too cheap a paper will make your books look shoddy (I have seen manuals printed on paper so thin you could see the print on the other side of the page) and will tear easily.

For your covers a variety of plastic and card options are available. If you are choosing ring binders, they come in a wide range of qualities from the cheap plastic folder with a single small pocket on the spine for the insertion of a card bearing the book's name, through those with a cloth covering on which details may be printed, to the top of the range padded leather binder the chairman would be happy to see sitting on his desk. Essentially your only constraint is cost - otherwise the sky's the limit!

Coloured inks can be used to great advantage in the printing process, although the costs do start to escalate. In this respect, it is essential you understand the terminology. One-colour printing is one colour on the paper, e.g. black on white (remember that grey is a shade of black). Two-colour is again, what it says. This might mean, for example, that you use black and one other colour to enhance diagrams. Four-colour, may sound modest or even mean, but is actually nearly the top of the range. The fact is, a four-colour specification (cyan, magenta, yellow, and black) gives the designer and printer an almost complete range of colour possibilities - the colours being mixed in different quantities and combinations to provide the full range of the spectrum. In addition you may specify special colours, possibly to meet a corporate colour requirement that must be completely accurate (for example, Coca-Cola® red), or a colour, such as gold or silver, the true form of which cannot be mixed from the four basic colours. Other modern materials such as laminates and foils can be used, but all add to the complexity and the cost of the process.

13.2 The considerations

So now you have an understanding of the options available to you and what has to be taken into consideration when making your choice. Obviously cost is always a major aspect and I outline below some of the factors which may affect this, but there may be other criteria that override mere cost considerations and these also deserve some thought.

13.2.1 Quantities required

At a basic level, small circulations generally dictate going down the photocopying road, since printing short runs pushes the cost of production beyond reasonable economic levels. At the other end of the scale there comes a point where printing is actually cheaper, although on single-colour production this might not occur until about 500 copies are required and considerably more than this figure on two-colour.

13.2.2 Maintenance requirements

If you use any of the binding methods other than loose-leaf ring binding, a book is not maintainable. The implication is that the book will be discarded when the new version of the software is installed. This, of course, is very expensive, but it looks good and displays a great deal of confidence on the part of the owner. It can also be the supreme example of the writer's attempt to produce a book that is the ultimate in user friendliness - a user guide that is perfect bound looks and feels just like any other book the user may have at home. If your book will never change or will always be produced in large quantities and issued only with system updates like many mass market personal computer products, this approach may be appropriate. If you, like me, are not afforded this luxury, read on.

Most books do change as products develop - new sections will emerge and others must change. This means that maintenance of the book is a serious financial factor in the decision about the production method. If maintenance *is* important, loose-leaf in one form or another is essential. Binders are much more expensive than gluing, but you only bear the cost of the binder once, and subsequent maintenance of a book in a binder is infinitely cheaper than reprinting the entire book every time. It is comparatively easy to issue instructions for the addition, substitution, and deletion of pages from an existing book, and appropriate page labelling can satisfy the requirements of even the most pedantic standards institution.

As use of even a second colour can double the cost of printing in a single colour (black), the need for maintenance generally dictates the use of a single colour for user manuals. Some use a spot second colour for headings and title pages, but the normal approach is to rely on good design to raise the quality of the book while keeping costs to a minimum. Photocopying a few pages is a great deal cheaper than printing, even on a long run, since the set-up costs of a print run are much higher than photocopying. Sometimes, therefore, the decision to print or photocopy at the outset may be decided by the likelihood of changed pages in low quantities on a fairly frequent basis over subsequent months and years.

13.2.3 Company image

Self-image is a very important factor in the production decision game. Many companies see the quality of their documentation as a hallmark, and they will go to endless lengths to produce to the highest quality whenever possible. If there is a precedent for high-quality production, it should be fairly simple to obtain sign-off for a continuance of this policy.

Of course, there is a difference between gaining a reputation for, as an example, beautiful four-colour brochures, and digging your hand very deeply indeed into your pocket to pay for a four-colour manual that is 98 pages long. As a consequence, it is quite common to find that manual production quality is just a little disappointing compared with the brochures that described the product to the prospective user.

There is, indeed, a psychological point in here which the writer might like to use. A well-prepared and expensive colour brochure describing a speculatively produced software package gives the reader two messages - the obvious one saying 'come and buy', and a subliminal one conveying the idea that this is a company that looks after its customers. As user guides are, by their very nature, read by a captive audience post-sale so to speak, a contrast between a beautiful brochure and a tacky manual may say something quite different to the product's user. It may say, in short, now we have got you, we are not going to try so hard.

The other way in which you may win this particular argument is to nobble the sales force. I know a number of instances where the eventual production quality was raised because the sales force wanted to use the manual in a pre-sales situation.

13.2.4 The audience

Another major factor that must be borne in mind when deciding on the best production approach to adopt is the requirements and aspirations of the audience. Very often the writer has a clearer view of this than the owner but, of course, the cost / benefit equation is not the highest priority in the writer's mind.

Audiences are impressed by quality. A sign in felt-tip pen saying 'mind the dog', does not have the same ring of authority as a brass plaque looking for all the world like the nameplate outside a solicitor's office.

This being so, the writer will be pushing for the adoption of a production process that exudes authority and adds to the majesty of his words. This works from the user's point of view also. A well-produced book which is easy to use will be treated with respect by most users, while a scruffy manual, A4 size and therefore too large for most working surfaces, held in a blue binder, will not impress or excite.

There may also be practical considerations. A book that will be used in a potentially dirty environment may need a cover that will either not attract dirt or can easily be cleaned. Similarly, if you are producing a quick reference card to be used in a hospital theatre, it may need a laminated surface.

13.2.5 Conclusion

Production costs can be surprisingly high. Whatever method is adopted, they all involve paper, ink, and labour, and these are all costs that are rising faster than inflation. The only things that put a brake on rising production costs are printers and print shops competing for work, and the advance of new technology which automates some of the processes.

Costs can be affected in a variety of ways, as described above. In addition, paper size can have an effect on the cost of printing. Printing equipment in this country is geared up to use paper of particular sizes. As I described in a previous chapter, selection of a non-standard page size will result in the printer having to trim the pages down to your specification. This will obviously incur additional cost for the paper wasted and the labour involved. As long as the European standards of A4, A5, and so on are adopted, all will be well, but a move to a size between these (which I prefer) may result in a sharp drawing in of breath and a shaking of the printer's head - all of which usually add up to megabucks for the owner. And this can affect your choice of binding too!

A major problem for the writer can be his inability to provide a firm estimate of print costs at the outset of the project. This is due to the fact that even if the owner is quite specific about the quantity required and the overall paper and colour specification, the writer cannot precisely predict how many pages he will need to use to explain the subject. However, it is usually possible to obtain a guide price based on a anticipated number of pages.

Printer's quotations tend to vary quite dramatically. This is due to commercial decisions the printer is making on a daily basis as he looks at the cost of his equipment and its utilisation. If you have plenty of time or the printer has not got much work on, he might slot your job in between other work and give you a special price as a consequence. Alternatively, if he is busy and you need your job in a rush, the costs may seem prohibitive.

All of the arguments provided in this section may be used by the writer in his attempt to get the very best frame put around his work of art. Most arguments will have to be pretty compelling, since the likelihood is that all suggestions will cost more than the owner would hope to spend. This is an argument for moderation and a practical solution rather than going for quality alone as a means to an end.

The arguments for quality are wrapped up in corporate well-being and pride, and the need to convey the authority and seriousness of the owner about the content of the books to the user family. If the owner has spent a large sum of money on production, he must be serious about the books and they should, for that reason alone, be read and adhered to.

The arguments for a practical solution are equally compelling. We have argued all along for books that work properly, and a production process that is practical continues that philosophy to the library shelf and the user's desk.

In the end, it comes down to a trade-off between quality and price. Hopefully, you, like us, will find one or two printers that you know can be relied upon to do an excellent job, on time, and within budget. Such are worth their weight in gold.

13.3 A note of caution

When appointing your printer, experience should be a factor in the cost equation. Some printers are not really suited to the production of a long document - earning their keep from brochures and one-page flyers. Printers will almost always all quote for a user guide job and, particularly if they are your existing supplier for brochures, they may provide you with what seems like a very reasonable price. However, you will not think it so reasonable if they do a poor job for you. You must be very careful when making your selection and remember that although a printer may be very good in his own field, he may not really be qualified or even competent to do your work well. If in doubt, you should always ask to see a sample of their work or ask for a reference from someone for whom they have performed a similar service.

13.4 Choosing whether to print in-house or externally

Your decisions here will probably depend on the extent of your in-house printing facilities. If the numbers to be produced are extremely large, the more automation and the less either the owner or the writer have anything to do with the process, the better. Printers will provide a number of ancillary services besides putting ink onto paper, and this can result in a product that, without further intervention, can land on users' desks. These services can include collating (putting the book into page-number sequence), drilling (putting holes in the paper for eventual location in a loose-leaf binder), the provision of tab cards or dividers (and putting these in the right places, too), shrink wrapping, provision and printing of binders, and even despatching to individual locations if necessary.

The photocopiers will also do some, if not all, of these processes, so, unless you have a printing department that can provide some or all of these facilities, there is a great deal to be said for opting to put the work 'out' where large quantities are involved. Certainly, poring over a hot photocopier in the general office at three in the morning when the collator goes down and 300 copies of a manual are required by 9 a.m. is an experience I would not like to repeat!

If your company does have printing or photocopying resources, you will need to ensure that they are capable of undertaking the work required. As with external printers, if they do not have sufficient experience or are not given adequate guidance, quality can be a problem. In addition, there is a tendency for internal printing departments to continue to use largely obsolete equipment long after it is life-expired. However, any drawbacks are usually more than compensated for by the sheer convenience of an in-house production solution. So long as the result meets the aspirations of the writer in terms of getting the message across, all parties should be happy and it is only where the company uses a drum duplicator and sees no reason to move forward from 1950s technology, that the owner and the writer are likely to fall out about production.

13.5 Print monitoring

Whichever print process is used, it is good to have someone who knows what they are doing monitoring the print process on behalf of the owner. The setting up for a printing run is quite a long task and may involve the overseer of the print process in checking proofs for quality prior to printing. For this we always use our designer, who has very considerable experience in this field.

If you are generating laser-printed camera-ready artwork, it is clearly your responsibility to check this for quality before sending it to the printer. When the camera-ready artwork is being generated from an electronic image setting process, you may ask for pre-print proofs to check the quality before the plates are made. Particularly when printing in colour, I would recommend that you do this. You will wish to check for quality - not of the words, as this will have already been done - but for the typographical quality of every character and line. That trained eye can be invaluable to spot fragmenting in type intensity which can result in a less than perfect book.

All this monitoring of printers and checking of proofs takes time and therefore money, but the investment is worthwhile for those books that warrant the very best of production processes.

14 Writing for export - is language the only problem?

The trend in business today is towards a world where international boundaries no longer exist. Software houses and large organisations rely more and more on international trade to secure increased turnover and higher profits.

Software houses can no longer assume long-term success on the basis of a product developed purely for a single nation and increasingly there is a willingness to look at products developed abroad before committing money to reinventing the wheel. Collaboration is the name of the game and many software houses carrying a range of products will have developed only a few of their 'lines' - the rest having been bought from other organisations - frequently based abroad.

In order to gain some control and vision concerning their international operations, many large conglomerates impose standard computer systems on their foreign subsidiaries. Usually these systems are sourced from one country and installed in many, and while there are certainly economies of scale as well as commercial benefits to be gained from standardisation, linguistic problems do arise.

14.1 The problems of language

There are few things more misunderstood than language. Furthermore, few of us would deny that the list of nations more ignorant than the British about languages, other than their own, is fairly short. As the modern writer is increasingly asked to face up to a requirement for text that can be used in other countries or translated into other languages, this chapter will endeavour to explore the problem and identify ways in which one can avoid at least some of the pitfalls.

Might we, perhaps, first look at language without concerning ourselves with the writing profession at all? Firstly, a few outrageous statements that I will try to substantiate - at least to my own satisfaction.

Even without the obvious barriers presented by the interaction of two languages, bad choice of words and misunderstanding what people say probably cause more divorces, litigation, strikes, and general unhappiness than any other single factor. It is clear from listening to conversations between people in all walks of life that a limited vocabulary, careless use of words, and an unwillingness to listen to what is being said, constantly mislead and misinform. Indeed, the very complexity of language and the subtle differences in meaning are used cynically by people to avoid issues or deliberately cause confusion. General elections provide wonderful examples of exaggeration and deliberate misleading on a grand scale and, from my apolitical standpoint, I obtain enormous pleasure, and pain, from listening to the accidental and intentional linguistic confusions made by our honoured leaders.

Language, while it is the basis of practically all human communication, is largely assumed and rarely studied in depth. It is so familiar to us that it breeds the ultimate in contempt. If we used it properly there would be no need to study it, but we do not, and I am quite sure that an Oxford don, marking this book for linguistic accuracy and precision, could write a highly critical report containing as many words as my original text. And yet I know that, on a scale of one to ten, I would probably rank a good three (one being top) while, taking the population as a whole, anyone who can make a living out of writing must be in the top one million in the nation. So we have a sad situation where those who can handle the language 'quite well' are exponents of the craft, while a growing percentage are becoming less articulate and, frighteningly, more illiterate every time statistics are published.

This is a problem and a great cause of sadness to those who see the language being destroyed more quickly than the proverbial Empire. It can also be a practical problem for the professional writer who seeks, at his own modest level, to achieve levels of linguistic quality that it is quite likely large sections of the audience are unable to appreciate.

If the English language is to be universally used - and this, fortunately for us, seems to be the only substantiable prognosis - what a sad thing it is that the nation from which it emanates, and which gave the language its name, is so ill-informed about its construction and use.

If English as an academic subject is rarely taught well - which can be the only conclusion one can draw from the present state of affairs - it is unlikely that foreign languages are taught well either. And this island race certainly has a reputation for ineptitude at speaking in tongues.

Why this should be the case is unclear. We are certainly no more stupid than, for instance, the Dutch - the vast majority of whom can speak at least two languages - Dutch and German - and many of whom will add English and French to their list as well. To find a Briton who is really competent in a single foreign tongue is a rare thing indeed, and the number who are truly familiar with four languages would probably not have to resort to standing on the first train through the Channel Tunnel. One factor may be that, for example, an understanding of French grammar would assume a prior understanding of English grammar and the teaching of grammar no longer holds a position of importance in most schools.

Another factor may be the switch to the teaching of languages at a conversational level. On the face of it, this would seem to be a positive step. After all, it is more important to be able to speak the language than to be able to write it and immersion in the language should result in the preparation of thousands of people for the only likely exposure they will have to the skill-need, which is when they go on holiday. Unfortunately, language is a dynamic thing - changing all the time, and the most conscientious teacher or tutor will lose a grip on current usage if he or she is out of the country for more than a few months.

Furthermore, the quality of conversation would have to be pretty impressive to reach a point where the vocabulary was stretched beyond the level of an Australian soap opera. Now this might be enough for buying a couple of beers in Munich, or even complaining that the brandy tasted like barbed wire in Marbella, but it is hardly learning the lingo and from the point of view of the technical author it is a thousand miles from translating a user guide successfully into another language.

One of the problems we have when comparing two languages is a basic misconception about language dictionaries. There they are, large and small, saying that 'this' word means 'that' in another tongue. Well, simplistically, it does, but dictionaries are unable to explain how the words are properly used in the real world.

Take two examples - both from French which, I should add, is my best foreign language. That is to say, I can carry on an intelligent conversation with a ticket clerk on the SNCF at a suburban station in the Paris region for about 25 seconds. Woe betide me if he should ask if I require the French Railways' equivalent of a one-day Capitalcard!

Firstly, the problem of direct translation of a single word. In English, the word 'serious' means two things - serious, as in 'a serious accident', and serious, as in 'he used to be very careless but has now become much more serious about his studies'. In French, the first definition would be represented by the word 'grave', while the second adopts the more obvious 'sérieux'. On closer examination of course, the two meanings are totally different and it seems quite sensible to use quite different words for them. Clearly, on this one example, the Englishman would show himself up and start a confusion of monolithic proportions with this error. Of course, the word 'grave' used to be used in the United Kingdom to describe an unpleasant event, but this seems to have subsided into disuse.

Then there is the coined-phrase problem. As an alternative to 'Good Morning' or 'Hello' (the French direct equivalent of which is only EVER used on the telephone), the English tourist or businessman abroad might be tempted to quip, 'What's new'? So, he looks up his dictionary and finds that 'What' is 'Quel', 'is' is 'est', and 'new' is (masculine) 'nouveau' So, trés simple, 'Quel est nouveau'? Non. Absolument, non. The French say, 'Quoi de neuf'? At least, that's what they say this week.

This dynamic redefinition of word meaning, of course, is not simply a condition of peoples in other nations. We are constantly changing the meaning of words in English too, and nowhere more than in youth culture. My twenty-year-old daughter seems to pepper her college conversation with the word 'cool', which generates a certain amount of, it seems, inaccurate déjà vu in me. Back in the fifties, 'cool' was applied by the emancipated youth of the time exclusively to music. Thus in a smoky jazz cellar someone would be described as playing a 'cool horn'. Nowadays, 'cool' seems to be used a great deal more, but it is a sort of encouraging interjection during a conversation given by the individual who happens not to be talking at nineteen to the dozen at the moment.

This is not only a factor for the language of the young, and I have in my possession a very interesting dictionary that lists innumerable words that have dramatically changed their meanings over the centuries. In our own times, the word 'totalled' has come to mean 'written off', 'joy rider' now means 'under-age vehicular potential murderer', 'I can see where you are coming from' means 'I understand', and so on. It is often difficult to understand what is being said in our own language - let alone handle the changes being made almost daily in a foreign tongue.

Another factor is an extraordinary arrogance that we, in the UK, still suffer from when it comes to languages. It is still possible to see tall, straight-backed English matrons in the cool reception areas of elegant hotels on the French Riviera sounding off in slow, loud, schoolmarmy tones at the nonplussed receptionist from north Africa who has not been exposed regularly to the Englishman (or woman) abroad. 'Speak slowly, loud, and in English (what else?), and they will jolly well have to understand' is a school of thought still practised widely.

This has been replaced in the younger generations by a scarcely concealed conceit about their prowess at languages. I have been so often in situations where people have volunteered to help me because they took French to 'A' level, only to find that I certainly understood more of what was going on, and by listening I was able to overcome the problem just as well as my erudite and slightly crestfallen companion. The excuses afterwards rank alongside those given by poor golfers who fancy themselves good but off-form. 'He was unhelpful - could tell I knew a bit of French, so decided to try to trip me up', is a favourite, but 'did you notice his broad Alsatian accent? Almost as difficult for me, knowing Rennes as I do, as a Bristolian in Glasgow', is always calculated to restore loss of face and make me impressed by his intimate knowledge of the intricacies of the language's regional accents. Sorry. It doesn't. Of course when you think you know it all, there is very little point in learning more and most Brits abroad think that they are better at languages than they really are.

14.2 Considerations when writing for translation

So where is all this leading to? To sum up so far, we do not understand English grammar, we cannot be taught French in the traditional way because we have not got a good grounding in our own language, the dictionaries, whilst essential, do not tell us how the language is actually used, and conversational language tuition is unlikely to progress beyond, 'What did you do at the weekend'?, 'Would you like to come to dinner with me'? and, 'This beer is rather warm for the time of year isn't it'?

Well, the writer of user guides may well be informed that his or her book is to be translated into French or Swedish or Mandarin Chinese. What, given our appalling record in the art of speaking with tongues, should the writer bear in mind and how do we overcome the snags discussed above?

Now it could be argued that this is just not the writer's problem. He, after all, has enough to do simply writing the books without having to worry about whether or not the book will translate well into French or whatever. That is the job of the translators - they have the skills and knowledge to sort that all out. Well this is true. And yet the final objective for the writer is that the book is read, and just because it has been translated on the way, it would seem churlish for the writer to wash his hands of his prime objective.

Translation is about words, meanings, and 'tone'. Many of the principles when writing for translation should be adopted as a matter of course in any writing project. Keeping things simple and unambiguous, and not using obscure words are policies that should be followed when writing any user guide. However, when writing for translation, there are some other things the writer must consider as well.

The first thing to remember is that the books must always use a precise 'international' English, without employing quaint English affectations. For example, avoid the use of 'and so on', 'on and on', 'rule of thumb', 'enter the screen' (difficult if you are more than a few inches tall). Although your English readers may appreciate and understand these, there will often not be an equivalent phrase in the destination language for the translation.

The writer should also avoid using phrases such as, 'the screen on the next page', or 'the diagram two pages on', or 'the instructions on the opposite page' in any text that may be translated. The reason for this is quite simple. As text is translated, it drifts from the pagination set up in the English version. On the whole, other languages take more space than English. This means that what was 'below' is now on the next page and a 'diagram two pages on' may now be about three pages away.

Desktop publishing constraints may also have an effect on all this, as a diagram that fitted neatly below a third of a page of text may now need to be moved on to the next page. Incidentally, I hope you noted an English-ism creeping into the phrases above. You should not say 'two pages on' as there will be guttural cries of 'two pages on what'? from Calais eastward. You might say, 'the next diagram', or if it is not next, resort to figure numbers. Many of you will say that in publishing 'below' and 'above' are used, precisely to avoid these sorts of problems. They are. In Britain.

14.3 How to manage the translation

Translation, as an industry, has a poor reputation - almost as poor as that of professional writers. It should be a major industry in these days of dismantled borders and prolific international trade, but it is not and language is still seen by many as the major inhibitor for pan-European business, for example. Often the companies that do trade abroad try to reduce their costs by avoiding using professional translators and getting down to the problem themselves.

If you have access to a foreign language speaker, this may seem like an ideal solution. But beware, life is not as simple as it seems!

I was recently shown a piece of French that had been translated from English by a well-meaning lady who, although French, had lived in the UK for about thirty years. The draft was beautifully written by hand. It was a moment or two before I realised that there was something odd about the text. Although the piece was quite long, there were no accents to be seen at all. Now, you don't even have to be able to buy your ticket at Louveciennes to know that the French are mighty fond of the odd grave, acute, circumflex, cedilla, and even the isolated umlaut. Not one to be seen. I pointed this out to my sceptical client, who much doubted the comments of an Anglo pitted against the assumed opinion of an undoubtedly French person, and I went away questioning my own sanity.

Such people, though very keen and willing, will inevitably be somewhat out of touch with their language of origin, and a two or three week holiday once a year is not sufficient to bring them up to date with the current trends in their language. Furthermore, in many cases they will be good at their language as spoken colloquially, but not aware of the terminology and phraseology used for the computer industry and the business area to which the book applies.

The conclusion one must inevitably come to is that professional translation is the only answer. But even the professionals, horror of horrors, can make mistakes. The writer will almost inevitably have to deal with the translators, and there are safeguards that can be introduced during the translation process that will avoid some of the pitfalls.

14.3.1 Preparing a glossary

The first thing to watch is words that must be translated in a particular way. Some computer terms, for example, are used in a very specific manner and must be translated as such. For example, you would not wish your references to 'fields' to be translated as meadows. Terminology is very important and, if mistakes of this kind creep in, the translated book will quickly be ridiculed and fall into disrepute. To prevent this from becoming an issue, before a full translation takes place, a glossary of technical and sensitive terms should always be prepared. These terms will include trademarks, product names, the names of hardware and software products, commercial, and computing terms. These should be translated (or, in the case of product names, not translated) and approved by the owner (and their foreign representatives) before full translation takes place.

I have already mentioned the word field in the context of computer systems. Some other words that you should watch out for are:

- computer (*ordinateur* in France, but almost always computer in other languages) and all other computing terms
- monitor - when you mean the terminal or screen
- boot and bootstrap
- menu
- manual
- figure - as in Fig. Nos
- Return
- Enter
- keyboard names in general
- data.

14.3.2 *The location of the translator*

You should be aware that, although some countries share languages, they are not always used in the same way. The one we can all relate to, of course, is the difference between English English and American English, but the same sorts of difference will apply to French French as opposed to Canadian French, and Brazilian Portuguese rather than the European variety. If you accept this tenet, it goes without saying that a book for use in Brasilia must be translated by a Brazilian, whereas one for Lisbon should be translated by a Portuguese.

When you combine this with what I said earlier about expatriates becoming out of touch with their native language, it becomes clear that translation should always take place in the destination country using people whose first language is the destination language. Now this is a real cruncher. Some translating organisations will skate around this one with all the skill and flamboyance of a finalist in the World Figure Skating Championships. If, however, you subscribe to even half of my observations on this subject, you will appreciate the need for this condition.

The expatriate angle cannot be too strongly expressed. Language changes so rapidly in such a variety of ways that the German wife of a man in the office who has been out of her native country for more than three years will already be beginning to lose touch with the language as it is actually used. These people still have a value as translators, but not at a technical level with the volume of work associated with user documentation. It is better to be safe than sorry and ensure that your document at least has a chance for real accuracy.

14.3.3 Reverse translation

If it can be afforded, selected passages from the book should be translated back into English - by a British person in the United Kingdom, of course. This will allow the writer to check that the 'tone' of the writing is as it was written, and ensure that it has not changed out of all recognition (see Figure 14.1).

Experience once again provides me with an illustration of why this is necessary. Some years ago, a friend had a document translated into Dutch. He did all the right things - it was translated in Holland by a Dutch national. The original document was a friendly, supportive piece - an overview or introduction. When selected passages were translated back into English, however, the tone had altered completely. The gentle 'welcomes' were gone, and the gentle, suggestive, style - more associated with feminine Japanese - had been bulldozed out of the way and replaced by an emphatic and dominating style. 'You will do this' replaced encouraging murmurings, and the whole thing was brutal and uncaring. The entire piece had to be translated again.

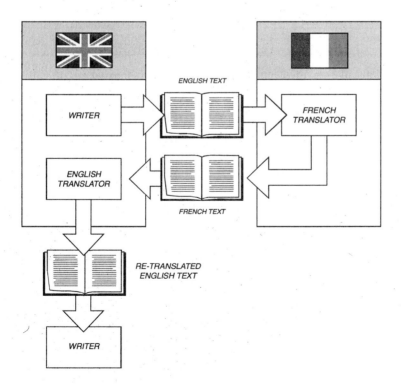

Figure 14.1
Reverse translation

14.4   Translating desktop-published books

As I said earlier, translation always changes the length of the text. If you desktop publish your books therefore, the text and diagrams will have to be relaid and adjusted on the pages after the translation is complete. Clearly this may be a difficult task if you are not familiar with the language, and you will want to make it as easy as possible. Many desktop publishing packages use a 'tagging' or 'mark-up language' coding system to identify text characteristics. If these codes remain in the text, it will make the desktop publishing exercise considerably simpler.

Most linguists nowadays are familiar with computer technology and translation is normally done on PCs. Wherever possible, you should leave the tagging or mark-up codes in the electronic file supplied to the translator and insist that the translator retains these in his translated text. This will mean that, although the writer and desktop publishing operator may not understand the translated text, it will be possible for them to find their way around and relate it to the original.

The desktop publishing of the translated text could, of course, be left in the hands of the translators, but you would have no control over the quality of the process. For this reason, it is a very good idea for final production control to be in the hands of the writer and desktop publisher. To leave this to the translators may be to court disaster.

There is one other point you should consider here. Captions, diagram annotations, headers, and footers will not always be part of the main text file for a book. It is essential that the translators receive a printed copy of the book as well as electronic files and that they are made aware of items that must be translated and marked on this hard copy.

14.5   Translation of illustrations

Do not forget that if diagrams and screen examples are used in your book (if not, why not?) these will need to be translated too. This can add significantly to the work and the cost. For example, diagrams should be fairly easy, as the drawing and, therefore, the redrawing to admit longer captions are probably completely under the control of the writing team. Screens (and reports) are a completely different kettle of fish, as you really cannot get them translated unless there is an intention on the part of the owner to translate the screens themselves. It would simply not do if you cleverly changed 'customer' to 'client' for a French version, only to find that a directive goes out to the effect that, to save costs, the screens will remain in English (and this happens frequently - incredibly).

There again, if translation of the screens is to be done, it would be better for the writer to wait until the software people have arranged this translation, and for him then to 'grab' new files of the translated screens to be incorporated into the book. This can be done after the text is translated, if necessary. The advantage of this approach is that, if the translation of the screens is done by a translator working with the software team, they have the problem of making the words fit properly beside the fields they represent, and can decide on appropriate abbreviations or alternatives. If the writer translates them, or get them translated, difficulties could arise meaning that the whole project could be severely delayed and the finger of suspicion might well end up pointing at the writing team.

14.6 Scheduling the translation

Translation - proper translation, that is - takes a while to accomplish properly and you should allow plenty of time for the process. Like writing, if it is rushed, it will be done badly and there is nothing worse than a poor translation.

If you allow enough time and if you follow the general advice discussed above, translation should hold few fears for you.

15 Conclusion

Writing a book about writing user documentation is, in some ways, a frustrating process. There is so much to say, and yet so little of what there is to say is at all scientific.

Of all the tasks connected with the computer industry, there are few as undisciplined as the writing process. This book tries to set a framework around the process that is rigid enough to maintain a degree of control, while at the same time leaving room for creativity and time to research the audience and product.

Similarly, few tasks associated with the computer industry are, frankly, as badly done as the writing process. While it is difficult between the covers of a book to provide a workable writing course - and this BCS Practitioner Series is not the place for such a tutorial - much can be improved if the problems are aired and discussed. The basic error of writing about the subject rather than the requirements of the reader has been stressed, as has the need for thought when books are to be translated.

A strong case has also been made for the replacement of long, dusty, manuals by a series of short books which hopefully will be read. It is always important for the writer to remember who his readers are and what they need from the books (see Figure 15.1).

Documentation is an essential and often unappreciated part of any software development project. The processes described here may seem lengthy and indeed you may feel that some of them are unnecessary. They are, however, what we have found best ensures the final quality. In the long run, the time and effort put into the development of good user documentation will reap dividends and save the owner company money by:

- reducing the amount of time spent handling queries and complaints
- increasing user satisfaction and understanding
- lifting the image of the company in the eyes of the users and potential users.

Inevitably, a work such as this one, that is so subjective, must contain the ideas and prejudices of one person - albeit edited by a number of supportive colleagues. There may, therefore, be aspects about which you do not agree. However, when all the chaff has been blown away, I hope that there are at least a few grains of true corn that may help you to write good user documentation or at least appreciate the problems that a simple scribe faces.

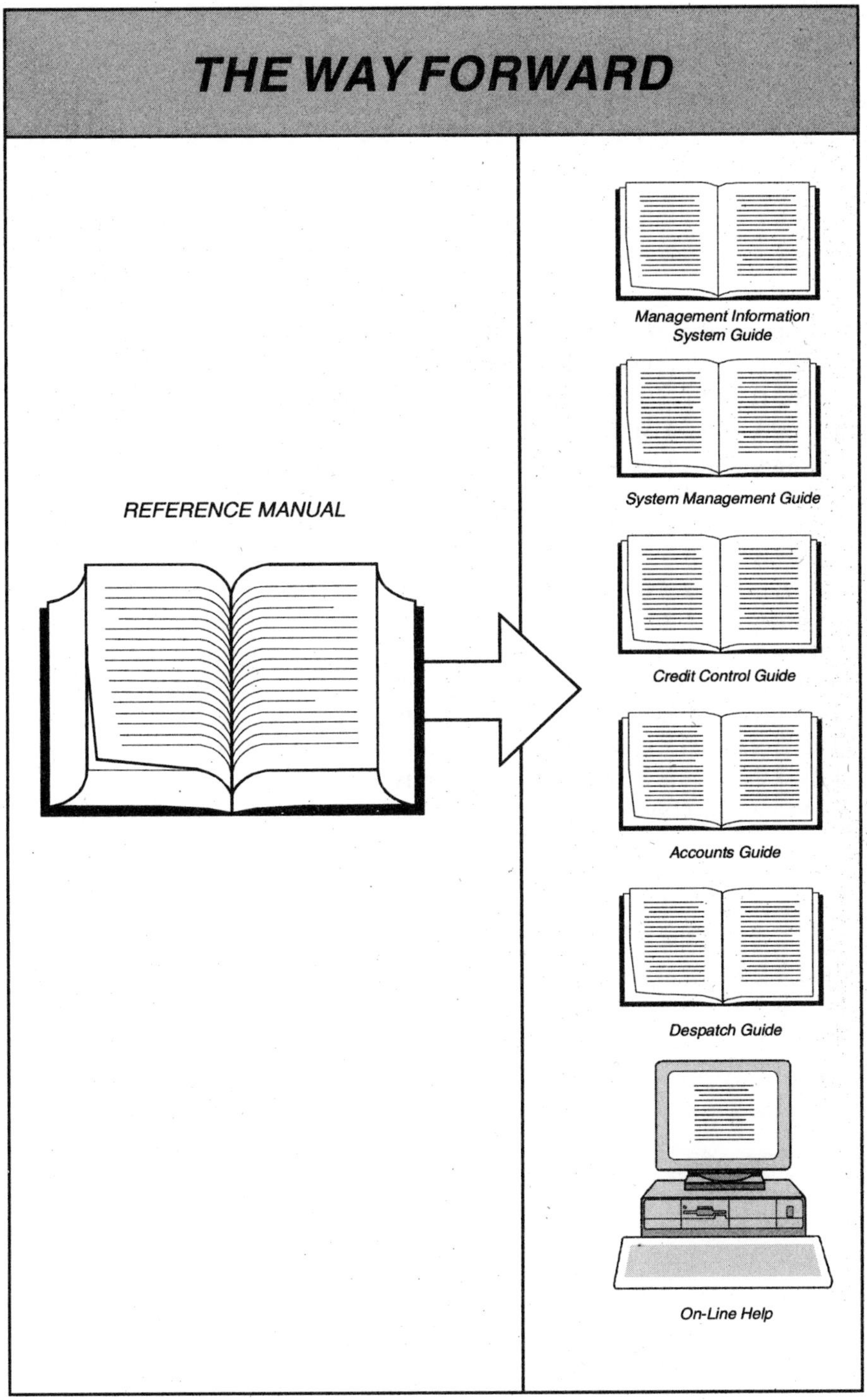

THE WAY FORWARD

REFERENCE MANUAL

Management Information
System Guide

System Management Guide

Credit Control Guide

Accounts Guide

Despatch Guide

On-Line Help

Figure 15.1
The way forward

Bibliography

Bann, D. (1986) *The Print Production Handbook*, Macdonald.

Barrett, E. (ed.) (1989) *The Society of Text*, MIT Press.

Barrett, E. (ed.) (1988) *Text, ConText, and HyperText*, MIT Press.

Bryan, M. (1988) *SGML: An Authors Guide to the Standard Generalised Markup Language,* Addison Wesley.

Marlow, A. (1990) *Good Design for DTP Users*, NCC Blackwell.

Murphy, H. and Hildebrandt, H. (1991) *Effective Business Communications*, McGraw Hill.

Rizk, A., Streitz, N. and Andre, S. (eds) (1990) *Hypertext: Concepts, Systems, and Applications. Proceedings of the European Conference on Hypertext, INRIA, France, Nov. 1990*, Cambridge University Press.

Sutcliffe, A. and MacCauley, L. (eds) (1989) *People & Computer V*, BCS Workshop Series, Cambridge University Press.

Vliet, J. van (ed.) (1986) *Text Processing and Document Manipulation*, BCS Workshop Series, Cambridge University Press.

Wahlstrom, B. (1992) *Perspectives on Human Communication*, William. C. Brown.

Glossary

A4/A5	Finished trimmed sizes in the standard range of metric paper sizes laid down by the International Standards Organisation and British Standards Institution.
Bullet-point	A device used to 'point-up' a short paragraph of text.
By-line	A line at the start of a book giving the author's name.
Comb binding	A book binding method that, with the use of a patent machine, permits updating of the volume.
Copyright	The exclusive right to produce copies and to control the publication of a book. This is granted by law for a specified number of years.
Designer	A person who devises and executes designs. When creating user documentation, the designer may either be a specialist book designer or the writer of the guide.
Desktop publishing	The process of using a computer system for electronic page make-up, incorporating typography and graphics. This often replaces the more traditional method of typesetting.
Draft	A version of a book that is under development.
Editor	A person who edits written material for publication. When preparing user documentation, two categories of editor are usually involved: the technical editor checks the technical accuracy of the text and the word-quality editor checks the quality of the language used. Naturally, a single individual may perform both functions.

Font	A set of type characters of the same design and the same size.
Glossary	An alphabetical list of terms peculiar to a field of knowledge, together with definitions or explanations. When documentation is to be translated, a 'translation glossary' must be prepared that identifies words that must be translated in a particular way.
Guide	A publication that instructs and explains the fundamentals of a computer system in business-oriented language.
Hard copy	Text that is presented on paper rather than on screen.
Hypertext	A computer database of text which may be navigated at high speed following the cognitive processes of the user. Hypertext allows a user to interact with the documentation in the way that best suits his needs at any given time.
Icon	A graphic symbol or small picture displayed on screen or on the printed page used to provide an easy way of identifying a feature or function. An example of the exclamation mark in a screen shown in Figure 6.3 on page 70.
Information CAGE	The Information Communication And Generation Expression. An illustration that shows how the flow of information in a business relates to processes taking place at different levels in the hierarchy of a business.
ISBN	International Standard Book Number. A unique ten-figure serial number that identifies the language of publication of a book, its publisher, and its title, plus a check digit.
Liability notice	Text that protects the owner and writer of a book from incorrect interpretation of the contents of the book.
Logo	A corporate pictorial image. A device that is used by companies on stationery and literature.
Manual	A book providing instructions or information about a system, usually phrased in system rather than business terms.

Multi-media	Systems that combines still images, video, still or animated graphics, text, and high-quality voice, music, or sound effects on a computer.
On-line documentation	Instructional text that appears on a computer screen.
Owner	The person or organisation with the overall responsibility for the publication of a document.
Pagination	The method and style of page numbering used in documentation.
Perfect binding	A book binding method that is permanent and does not permit updating of the volume. Perfect binding is used in paperbacks.
Quick reference card	A small card or booklet proving a fast reminder about key areas of a system.
Reference documentation	Documentation in the form of a manual, usually organised alphabetically or in system-menu sequence.
Reviewer	The person or persons ultimately responsible for checking the accuracy and completeness of text produced by a writer, and for providing corrections and additions to the text where appropriate.
Styleguide	A document defining rules and examples of writing style, punctuation, typography, etc., for the use of writers, editors, and desktop publishers.
Synopsis	A brief overview of a document providing essential details about its structure and content.
Trademark	The name or other symbol used to identify goods produced or marketed by a particular manufacturer or dealer, and to distinguish them from goods produced by competing manufacturers and dealers.
User	A person using a computer system to assist them in performing their normal business activities.

User documentation	Computer system documentation that is couched in business terms and structured in a manner appropriate to the way in which a user operates the computer system in their normal business environment.
Visual	An accurate interpretation of how one perceives an end product, incorporating all the different design elements. Shown early in the process of production of documentation.
Warranty notice	A statement indicating the level of warranty provided by the owner of a system and its documentation.
Wiro	A binding method using continuous wire turned into a spiral. This method does not allow for updating of the volume.

Index

'Angara', 2
annotation, 80
American Constitution, 3
appendices, 106
attributes, 74
audience, 21
avoiding repetition, 92

'Baikal', 2
binding, 143
book,
    authority of, 34
    ownership of, 38
    structure, 48
    working model, 63

CAGE,
    description, 10
    (illustration), 11, 24, 33
chapters, 50
choosing your printer, 149
clip-art library, 79
collating, 150
column (illustration), 69
colour printing, 145
comb binding, 143
combined indexes, 103
computocash, 8
contents sheet,
    description, 100
    (illustration), 101, 102
copyright notice, 98
corporate colour, 146
corporate design standards, 65
corrections, 120

data in correct file format, 77
design creation, 67
designer,
    work of, 65
    working with, 139

desktop publishing,
    description, 12
    operators, working with, 139
diagrams, 19, 75
dictionaries, 89
dividers, 150
document size, 66
documentation budgets, 4
drafting process, 83
drilling, 150

editing,
    description, 111
    appearance and layout, 114
    policies, 111
    processes (illustration), 137
    spelling, 119
    for word quality, 118
editor's marks (illustration), 121
electronic manuals, 37
end matter, 102
errors, 12

field-sensitive help, 40
final draft preparation process (illustration),
    136
first draft,
    preparation process (illustration), 135
    review, 128
fonts, 71
footers, 72
four-colour specification, 146
flowcharts, 79
front matter, 45, 97

glossary,
    description, 102
    for translation purposes, 157
'grabbing' software, 77
graphic surround (illustration), 78
graphics, 73

'Greek', 63
grid,
    description, 69
    (illustrations), 69, 70
gutter (illustration), 68

headers, 72
Heath-Robinson, 104
hypertext, 40, 42

illustrated description, example, 61
illustrators,
    working with, 139
illustrations, 94
image, 147
indexing,
    description, 103
    main entries, 105
    sub-entries, 105
Information CAGE,
    description, 10
    (illustration), 11, 24, 33
interviewing,
    appropriate, 18
    failure in, 17
introductions, 50
investigation,
    conduct of the, 34
    the method, 31
    two stages, 20

jargon, 23

keyline surround (illustration), 78

Lake Baikal, 2
liability notice, 99
loose-leaf binding, 143

main text,
    description, 48
    structure, 48
maintenance, 147
management, 132
managing translation, 157
margin (illustration), 68
mark-ups, 86
measure of writer effectiveness, 31
Mr. Men books, 94
multi-media, 40

non-computing activities, 56

on-line text, 39
owner confidence, 124

page size, 68
pagination,
    by chapter, 50

by section within chapter, 50
    general description, 49, 50
    sequential, 50
Panama Canal, 3
paper quality, 145
perfect binding, 143
person, second or third, 45
personal editing, 107
Pirelli calendar, 8
point size, 71
preface, 48, 100
preliminary,
    discussions, 125
    editing, 107
print methods,
    description, 142
    externally, 150
    in-house, 150
print monitoring, 150
printing,
    cost of, 148
    description, 143
problems of using on-line help, 40
production,
    methods (illustration), 144
    stages, 83
productivity, 109
project,
    liason, 140
    stages (illustration), 85

quality issues, 147, 148
question and answer techniques, 52
question section, 53

'read', 118
reading technique, 37
repetitions, 107
reports,
    description, 75
    showing live data, 77
reproduction,
    restrictions, 47
    volumes, 146
reverse translation, 159
review,
    arbitration, 86
    targets, 126-131
reviewers,
    description, 84
    change of, 141
reviewer's role, 125
rules for reviewers, 126

sales order processing in a mail order
    company, 26
sans serif type, 71
scheduling, 136
screen, 75

screen-sensitive help, 40
screen surrounds (illustration), 78
second draft,
    preparation process (illustration), 135
    review, 129
serif type, 71
shelved projects, 133
short books, benefits of, 25
shrink wrapping, 150
sign-off documents, 125
spell-checkers, 107
'spinal' knowledge, 6
stapled binding, 143
Statue of Liberty, 3
Sterne, Laurence, 15
stitched binding, 143
structure, 48
style, writing, 92
styleguides,
    description, 44
    preparation of, 54
sub-headings, 74
symbols,
    description, 60, 94
    (illustration), 61
synopsis,
    contents of, 44
    description, 43
    review, 127
sympathy writing, 22
synonyms, 89

tab cards, 150
targeted user, 21
technical edit, 116
technical editor's checklist, 117
technical terms, avoidance of, 93
technical writer, a misnomer, 14
technoanxiety, 22
technospeak, 5
telephone sales, 28
temperament, 90
tense, 16
text tweaking, 81
theme park leaflets, 100
titling of books, 32, 54
tolerance in the search, 101,
trademarks, 47, 100
training, shortcomings, 7
translation,
    glossaries, 157
    management, 157
    of desktop-published books, 160
    of illustrations, 160
    problems, 152
Tristram Shandy, 15
turgid text, xii
type size, 71
typefaces, 71

user,
    anxiety, 22
    general description, 21
user documentation,
    driven by user need, 38
    reputation, 1

visuals, 63
voice, 45
warranty notice, 47, 99
welcome message, 48, 100
white space, 68
wiro binding, 143
word,
    choice, 92
    overpopulation, 93
word-processed manual,
    example of, 55, 56
word-quality editing (illustration), 120
work centres, 136
writer's,
    block, 108
    'boss', 31,
    productivity, 109
writing, a collaborative process, 125
writing,
    style, 45, 92
    tools, 89